Jonny Kennedy

The Story of the Boy
Whose Skin Fell Off

as told to
Roger Stutter

tonto press
www.tontopress.com

ISBN-13: 9780955218385

British Library Cataloguing in Publication Data: A catalogue record for this book is available from the British Library

Thanks to Nell McAndrew, Edna Kennedy and Marianne Lund

Photographs courtesy of Edna Kennedy except where stated

Front cover photograph Andy Lamb / Evening Chronicle

Printed and bound at Athenaeum Press Ltd,
Gateshead, Tyne & Wear

Tonto Press

Newcastle upon Tyne

United Kingdom

www.tontopress.com

I dedicate this book to all sufferers of Dystrophic Epidermolysis Bullosa, to all sufferers of other forms of EB, and to all their carers.

Roger Stutter

Foreword

by Nell McAndrew

I WILL never forget the day I first met Jonny. I had agreed to help support the DebRA charity by taking part in a photo shoot with several children who had EB and their families. We were going to release butterflies as a symbol of the delicate skin of someone who has the condition. At the last minute I was told there would be a man there called Jonny who wanted to meet me.

The event was in Hyde Park, London, and the sun was shining, not a cloud in the sky, a perfect day. I didn't know what to expect or what I was going to say to any of the people there, especially Jonny as he was older. I mean, what do you say to someone who has had to go through so much and knows that he is dying? I needn't have worried though, because from the moment I introduced myself to him and we started chatting it was like we had known each other for years.

Jonny was very open about his condition, and wanted to share his experiences. He was very articulate, funny, charming – and a bit cheeky as well! I thought I was controlling my emotions well, until he started telling me that he missed being cuddled. His severe form of EB meant that a simple thing like a cuddle could cause him so much pain, discomfort and even blistering. I couldn't hold back my tears any longer, and began to cry. I gave him a cuddle, very gently. I could never, ever imagine what he had had to cope with all his life. After I left him that day, I couldn't stop thinking about him.

Jonny had invited me to his house warming party. He had given me his card with his address and phone number on, with the date written on the back so I wouldn't forget when it was. I was determined to be there no matter what. In the meantime, Jonny and I kept in touch by text and occasional phone calls. The party was brilliant. His family were there, it was lovely to meet them, and his brother cooked up a great barbecue!

That day, I told Jonny I was going to run the London Marathon to help raise more awareness and funds for DebRA, along with my other charities including Cancer Research UK, and that he had to be at the finish line for a cuddle! Unfortunately this wasn't to be, as Jonny died before the marathon took place. I did complete the run, with tiger tattoos on my arms in his memory. I burst into tears at the finish as I thought of him. I was also running for my dad who had been diagnosed with cancer and had recently undergone chemotherapy treatment. It was a very emotional day.

Jonny's mum, Edna, was there though, and she presented me with a gift that Jonny had left for me before he had died. It was a pretty necklace with a star pendant and a message that read, 'Friends are like stars, they don't need to be seen to know they are always there. Love, Jonny.' Well that was it – I burst in to tears!

Not a day goes by without Jonny being in my thoughts, and the number of people who are now aware of Jonny and EB is incredible. I feel very fortunate to have met such a special person, and I will never forget him.

Nell McAndrew

Introduction
by Roger Stutter

T HIS is the story of my friend Jonny Kennedy, written over a long period of time, whenever he had the energy to talk to me. It is the story of an extraordinary life, tragically short, but lived to the full. Jonny died before we could finish the book together, but I've done my very best to finish it for him. Those who knew him say he shines out from its pages.

Jonny was born on November 4th 1966 with the debilitating disease Dystrophic Epidermolysis Bullosa, a condition that was slowly turning him into a ball of twisted flesh. He existed on this planet without one moment of painless life for almost 37 years. Yet through all the suffering shone a clear bright mind and an unbelievably strong character who wanted to learn, to interact with people, and to have lots of fun on the way. Ultimately, Jonny just wanted to party.

To understand Jonny Kennedy you have to suspend your belief in what a human actually is, for Jonny did not live life like you or I, and didn't see things the way ordinary folk see them. How could he? He never experienced many of the things ordinary humans take for granted: driving a car, getting a job, having relationships, having kids, even simple pleasures like strolling in the countryside or swimming in the sea. None of these things were for Jonny.

Yet in the midst of all that was horrible emerged a sharp mind, inquisitive nature and fun personality that, in a remarkable way, has healed many across the globe. That was Jonny, and I hope that, in completing this book for him, I have done my friend proud.

Roger Stutter

Freedom

THE day has finally arrived. Ever since the glider flight was first mentioned I've been excited. Because for the shortest of times, for a few special minutes, I'll be free.

I'd like to say I got up early, but getting up early is not a Jonny Kennedy concept. I did notice, while my carer was attending to me, that the sky was a pure crystal blue: a beautiful summer's day. I wish my friends could be with me today, sharing this adventure. But there's only room for one lucky person up there and, for once in my life, that one lucky person is gonna be me.

I usually have the patience of a brick, with no need to hurry, but not this morning. I'm raring to go. Even though I have to take my time, and things like dressing and getting out of bed have to be done slowly, I'm eager to get ready and get going.

When I'm ready I'm stuffed with so much padding beneath my clothing I look like I weigh about 20 stone. I'm carried into the garage, then placed into my chair, which I manoeuvre into the back of the van to be clunk-clicked for the trip. I'm tied into place, and then we're off.

To my surprise the disused airfield we're heading to isn't all that far away, so we're there before the discomfort of the journey starts to bother me. My heart is beating almost as fast as it does when I think of Father, although it's excitement rather than anger that's getting my blood pumping today.

The glider, a smooth, engineless piece of art, sits in a field with a wing tip touching the grass. The pilot, professional and assuring, smiles as I joke with him to calm my nerves. Then I'm lifted, fitted into the cockpit, wished 'good luck' and left alone with the pilot, ready for take-off.

The glider is hooked up to a wire rope. Everyone stands clear. My breath is coming short and fast as the wire is pulled taut and, like a slingshot, *whoosh*, we're flying. I don't feel scared, only exhilarated. All I can hear is the sound of the air as we slice through it and climb into the huge, blue, open sky. The pilot pulls at a lever, the wire rope falls away, and we're on our own and free.

It's the freest I think I've ever been, and it's great. A

'Yippee!' escapes my lips as we turn, and a 'Wayhaaay!' as we swoop down. Sitting behind me, the pilot calls out points of interest on the land below, but, as beautiful as the land is, it's the sky that fascinates me as we duck and dive with nothing but air currents in our way. A sigh involuntarily leaves my lips, because I want to eat it all. To grasp it and hold it tightly to my chest. But such a call for freedom, sadly, I cannot heed. And although it seems to last a life-time, it does come to an end. And, as we *whoosh* back to-wards the ground, I'm so contented that even the bumpy landing doesn't hurt.

We're back in the real world, and people crowd around. I'm unplugged, carefully unhooked, lifted out, then pam-pered over. I thank the pilot – I only wish we could have stayed up there longer. When I die and my spirit is free I'll be back up there, playing with the angels, getting them off their little clouds, doing drops of a thousand feet and then pulling up, spicing things up a bit for them. But, hey, this was a good day for Jonny Kennedy, I can tell you that.

The day ends back home in my private little world, where I have to mark it, as I mark all my special days, with one of my favourite cigars. I mellow over a large glass-worth of brandy, daydreaming of those thrilling moments of freedom, which were mine such a short time ago.

Chapter One

DARK clouds gather outside and there is a sense that it is going to rain, although that doesn't matter to me as I lie cosy in my bungalow, brandy and cigars by my side. My name is Jonny Kennedy, and I am a 36-year-old man. God knows how I have lived this long. I'm approximately five feet tall, squashed and so crunched up by my condition. I'm a small, hairless, bandaged human being. The whole day has been spent lying around and relaxing, watching TV, drinking alcohol, smoking the odd cigar and just chilling out. Today is what I call a 'dossy day'. A day on which I do absolutely nothing. A day for psyching myself up in preparation for whatever the morrow will bring.

A few brandies later and I am relaxed. Tomorrow is tomorrow, but what of today? What a life, if you could call it that. Why am I the way I am? Why do I have to suffer all the time? What is it all about? Why me? All questions I've heard many ask of themselves. But today it is my turn, and I ask them of myself.

To answer them, though, I need to travel a long way back. So stay with me – and you will need all your courage and understanding on this journey. All of your emotions will be exercised by the story of Jonny Kennedy, I can promise you that. But stick with it, for you will learn a lot, too. In fact, we will both learn together. So let me begin by explaining why I need 'dossy days' and alcohol. Apart from the fact that I enjoy them, of course.

Dystrophic Epidermolysis Bullosa (EB for short) is the condition I suffer from, and it has been the bane of my existence from day one. I have very soft skin due to the fact that there is no 'glue' between the layers leading down to my flesh. So when my skin is banged or knocked it just comes away or blisters, which causes sores and huge scabs to form. This can – and does – happen all over my body, and inside my body, too, in my mouth and throat. As I'm sure you can imagine, the red-raw flesh sores are unbelievably painful. Even after 36 years, it's still difficult to get your head around the severe pain.

The chances of being born with EB are something like 1 in 300,000. Both parents must carry the faulty gene, and if they pass that down you'll end up with my condition. I like to think of my skin as being like Velcro, only with some of the hooks missing. So any bumps or friction pull the skin off. And then you're knackered.

Even if I knock myself gently, fluid will appear between the flesh and the skin. The fluid is a salty mixture, a bit like sea water. Pure protein, they tell me, which my body is losing all the time. I have to burst these blisters, otherwise the fluid will build up and the blisters'll spread and get bigger, sometimes stretching up to six inches across, and pulling what little skin I have away from my flesh. So I have to burst them, which is agonising and so delicate. Then the area has to be bandaged, because it's just raw flesh open to the air. If it was left unbandaged I would become one huge, hard, encrusted scab, and would be in horrific pain every time I moved. And believe me, I've been there and it's not a pretty sight.

I suppose I do look a little bit different from the norm. I don't know who Norm is, but I look a little bit different to him. A lot of people ask me if I've been burnt when they see me. I guess that's what it looks like to them, since I'm covered in sores and almost totally bandaged. You might have seen me around, in my electric wheelchair and white cap. A lot of people comment on my cap. It's become a bit of a trademark for me. Quite a fashion-setter, I am!

The pain caused by my condition is almost always too

much to bear, and the illnesses and diseases you can pickup without skin to protect you are endless. Once bandaged, it's a case of waiting for the affected area to heal. This takes a long time because the new skin is not the same as normal skin. It's very much like tissue paper or filo pastry and comes away with extreme ease, causing even more problems. Things happen to me spontaneously too, without me having to knock myself. Often it depends on my blood pressure or the way I'm resting. I'm sitting on my backside most of the day, so I'm prone to blistering more there. I seem to have had blisters and sores on my bum, some as big as a saucer, every day of my life. And I always have to lift my feet when I'm sitting, otherwise they'd get covered in blisters too.

And then there are my hands, which everyone can see. When I get a blister, say on the end of my finger, the skin tightens around it pulling the finger down towards my palm. Then, wishing to go to the aid of the blister, the skin on my palm takes the shortest route and jumps across from my hand to the tip of my finger, sticking them together. I wake up the next morning, after the healing process has done its worst, to find my fingertip wrapped in skin and attached to my hand. It's stiff, and I can't move it because it hurts. Next, I'll get a blister between my fingers, and the same process happens there, so they also end up joined together, and on and on. Before long, my whole hand is cocooned in blistering and peeling sore skin. If you look closely you can see my little fingers, nails too, trapped in a sheath of scorbutic flesh and scaly skin.

Today my hands are all crunched up and misshapen because of all the knocks and bashes I've given them over the years, but I've fought it as much as I could. I'm right-handed so, bent, twisted or sore, I try to force my right hand into action to write, eat or do other work. My wrists are permanently bent now, too, because I've had sores there which pulled my hands down to join them. And it goes on. In fact, wherever there is a crease on my body I have the same problem. My elbows, knees, armpits, neck, and even my ears – they all behave like my fingers, pulling and joining together. It's as if I am slowly being fused into a ball.

My underarms are affected, too, permanently sore and stuck together. Which means that I can't put my arms above my head. If I was involved in a bank robbery and they said, 'Put your hands up!' I'd be a goner!

Some people with this condition have operations on their hands to straighten them out, which means six months at a time wearing splints. And it never lasts for long – their fingers soon start closing in again. I know what I'm talking about. When I was very young I had two operations on my hands, but they weren't successful. They only did a few fingers at a time, and I had all those months in splints and all that trauma to deal with. They wanted to continue to do more operations, but I wasn't prepared to go through it all again just to have my fingers return to being trapped. No way. Plus it was a lot of trouble for my parents who couldn't get through to the hospital to see me every day, which meant I had to handle the hospital staff all by myself. It was just too much for me, maybe because I was just a young child, I don't know. But the nurses and doctors didn't take any notice of me. They thought they knew it all, but they didn't. It was a rough time for me then, and I didn't enjoy it at all.

Some sufferers have bother with their feet, which can end up as bad as their hands. It just depends on how much pain you can put up with. I mean, some people have sores on their feet and that's them laid up. But if you want to get about you have to just get on with it and keep walking, which is what I've always tried to do. I have blisters on my feet and they hurt like hell, but I've always done my best to get around. I mean, I'm not gonna just sit here and say, 'Oh dear, blisters on my feet,' and let them crunge up like my hands. Of course I rely a lot on my wheelchair these days. No matter how hard you fight it, you cannot stop it forever.

My decrease in mobility hasn't happened overnight. It has been a slow and inevitable process, and I've had to adapt according to what I can and can't do. Every day is a new challenge for me. Each morning I wake up wondering how I am going to be able to do ordinary things, like getting out of bed or getting dressed. I've had 36 years of this now, and it gets harder every day.

So my arms and my legs are also slowly being pulled up beneath me, and it's the same with other bits of my body. Anywhere that doesn't have to be stretched or used will knit together – even my ears. When I was younger I had sticky-out ears, a bit like Prince Charles. But, because of the sores there, my skin has pulled them in. I suppose I've done my own face lift!

I'm joking about face lifts, but the sores tighten my skin so much that if I live to be a hundred (God forbid) I'll never get wrinkles. That's why I still look like a young boy. As for hair, I don't think I went through full puberty as any normal teenager would. I think my body felt it wasn't needed. It must have had enough to do coping with all the skin problems without my hormones kicking in. Everything has just sat still with regard to hormones. That's why I don't have hair on my face, and have a high-pitched voice. It never broke. Physically, I'm still a young boy.

If I had facial hair I couldn't shave it, for obvious reasons, and if I got a sore on my face, which I would, there'd be a kind of matted mess amongst the hair, and it would be weeping, too. Pretty gross, eh? I'm glad in some ways that puberty didn't happen to me. I mean, I'm not worried about girlfriends and that sort of thing. I've never got involved in relationships, because I don't think it would be fair on the other person to have to deal with everything I have to deal with.

I do have a high-pitched voice, and if I answer the phone people are always mistaking me for Mother, but I can live with that. It's only when I'm out in the town that it gets to me. It amazes me, really, the amount of people who mistake me for a girl. If I go into a shop in my wheelchair, or into a lift, parents always tell their kids, 'Let the lady past.' And it's always the parents who make the mistake. If it's their kids who see me first they ask, 'Why is that man like that?' They never mistake me for a woman. So if I could have facial hair, I would like a moustache, because women don't normally have those. Then people would get it right.

Our family never had great heads of hair but, because of the condition, mine has mostly gone already. Sores and scabs on my head have slowly ripped out my hair at the roots. I only have a little bit of hair left, but that's actually a Godsend as it means there is less to get matted from sweat and sores. I have to bathe my head in the mornings to un-matt my remaining hair. It's horrible, but if I didn't do it my whole head would be clotted with gunge. I keep on top of things as much as I can, but it's a nuisance.

That's why I wear the white cap to cover my head, and I don't take it off in public. That suits me. I wouldn't say I worry about what people think, but I wouldn't like to upset anyone. Not that it looks gross, but I feel that, in certain circumstances, looking at me with my cap off could be quite shocking. It's a white flat cap and people recognise me by it, even though they don't know why I wear it, or what it covers up. Anyway, it's a North East tradition to wear a flat cap, and I like it.

I do have some clear-ish areas on my body. My ribs, stomach and chest are the best because my arms protect them. But that just means that, if I'm in a crowd, my arms get it. Everywhere else gets sores, even my face. When I lie down it puts pressure on the side of my head and ears and I end up with spots, which transform into blisters, before turning into sores and hard scabs. My life is, and always has been, a never-ending story of pain and bandaging.

There are creams and stuff that some people with EB find helpful, but I don't use any. I find they keep the sores wet, which only delays the healing. I just use dry gauze dressings, swabs and bandages. Putting on creams and other potions doesn't seem to help at all. I tried them when I was younger, because you try anything at that age to ease the condition. But as I got older I learnt that a lot of things made the condition worse, so I'd end up having more to put up with. I found it better to leave them alone and just try and get on with my life. I don't attempt things anymore unless I know they are going to work. I'm afraid I wouldn't be the best guinea pig in the world when it comes to testing things for other sufferers. Someone else will have to do that.

I've been a guinea pig before and, I can tell you, I won't be again.

They put me on cortisone when I was a boy. It was supposed to be the wonder drug of the age and was going to help swallowing and heal the skin and all sorts of things. I was on twelve tablets a day, and it nearly killed me. I had water retention, I was off my food, and I couldn't travel. The slightest motion made me sick, and I blew up like a balloon. I was longer coming off the damn things than I was actually on them. It was a nightmare. These days, if it's not proven, I'm not gonna touch it. It's down to other folk braver than me to do it now.

I've tried painkillers, but they don't work. It doesn't seem to matter what drug I take, I just seem to come out in a sweat. Doctors won't have it, but Mother has seen what the drugs do to me. Things like Aspinol or Panadol or whatever are supposed to bring fevers down, but they don't work with me. So far there has been only one thing that's worked, and I'm sure that was only because it put my attention elsewhere. A few years ago they put me on large doses of morphine, which sent me into a kind of stupor. I was hallucinating and talking to myself as if there was someone else in the room, but I didn't feel it got rid of the pain in the way I imagined. Morphine took me to a world of my own where I just forgot about pain. It blew my mind. The dosage was too high, plus it bunged my bowels up. I was really glad to come off it.

I'm in pain all of the time. But when I'm outside, in public, I'll have my 'mask' on. I'll be acting out a role, even though my leg – or whatever else – is giving me hell. I'll just get on with it, that's what I do most of the time. People ask, 'Are you in pain, pet?' and it's only then that I think about it and – oh shit! – I remember that it hurts. If they kept quiet it wouldn't be on my mind, and I'd be able to get on. People say these stupid things and they don't realise what it's doing to me. I'm in constant pain, and I've never known anything different. You're born with a headache, so what's a headache? You don't know because you were born with it. It's a bit like that. As soon as you're made aware of something, you can't get it out of your head.

Let's get back to the drugs, though. I'm sure that if you don't take them your body comes up with its own defences. I think the body creates its own 'morphine', which has got to be better for you than the stuff the doctors give out. Eventually, your brain stops receiving the messages of pain. Kind of switches itself off. Seems to, anyway. Keeping your mind occupied seems to be the best way to achieve this. Meditation works as well, that gets me relaxed. Sometimes I take myself away to imaginary places, just for a few minutes at a time, peaceful places. It's just a way of putting up with the pain and getting on with it.

I also have to watch what I eat. Due to the condition my

stomach has a slower digestive rate, so what I send down has to have a lot of nourishment in it, otherwise it doesn't get digested and I end up with internal bleeding. I'm supposed to have my daily roughage to keep me regular, but I don't have any because going to the toilet is an event in itself and can take up to an hour. Even my insides get blistered, and I end up bleeding when I go, which is a bit of a do. But there's nothing I can do about it.

Itching is another thing that bothers me. It's another form of pain, and it's something that is with me all of the time. I can't sleep at night because of it, and I can't scratch it either. The itch is usually on my back, and my only form of relief is to pat it with my crunched-up hand. That's what sends me to sleep – I become hypnotised by the patting until I drop off. Or maybe I fall asleep from exhaustion. Whatever, it's not unusual for me to continue patting in my sleep.

I was fast asleep one afternoon when Father knocked on the window. 'I knew you weren't asleep,' he told me later, 'because I saw you patting your back.' Of course I was asleep, but I was on autopilot. I think I'd be awake all the time if I stopped patting myself when I fell asleep.

So I don't sleep well. Most people can turn over in their sleep, but if I turn over it's a major exercise. My bandages stick to the bed, my head sticks to the bed, and I wake up. So I cat-nap more than anything. Some nights I can lie all night without falling asleep. As I can't eat properly, my blood levels aren't what they should be, and I tire easily. You see, I can't eat things that make iron – which your body needs for blood production. I take a supplement but, as you can imagine, I'm losing blood all the time from my sores, or going to the toilet, or even just eating. A blister might form as I eat, and I'll be bleeding in my mouth, but I just have to carry on regardless. Seems endless doesn't it? And it is. Nosebleeds are another thing I have to put up with. If I blow my nose too hard there is always a lot of blood loss. Unfortunately, my body can't keep up with what's needed to keep me alive, so blood transfusions are what I need.

Once, when I was about 19, I went to the doctors to complain about a pain in my side and was admitted to hospital for a major blood transfusion. I only had about four pints of the stuff left in me. The lowest amount a body can have, apparently. And guess whose blood just happens to be rare? Yes, lucky old me.

So that's the condition: Dystrophic Epidermolysis Bullosa. One hell of a mouthful, isn't it? Talking of mouthfuls, let me tell you about mine. Dentists are not my favourite people. I was in hospital a couple of times as a boy having extractions, and they always took out far more than they should have. What a mess they left me in.

My mouth is small, too, and it's getting smaller. You know what it's like when you get chapped lips and get sores on the sides of your mouth? With me, my skin grows over the sores. So, you see, my mouth is contracting, getting smaller all the time. It won't shut altogether because I use it too much. (I know, *I know*...) But it is a lot smaller than it was. I remember, when I was younger, I could put a Malteser in my mouth without any trouble. Now when I get a Malteser I have to eat it like an apple. I have to nibble bits off it until I can get it into my mouth. That's how small my mouth has become.

My teeth are very awkward. I can't brush them in the normal way or I'd damage my delicate gums. It's very difficult to maintain them, and I know a lot of people with the same condition who have lost their teeth altogether. In that respect I am very fortunate. Father was once a dental technician, and he knew that smoking helped kill bacteria. He smoked a pipe and cigars and, from when I was just four years old, he would let me have the odd smoke in the evenings before I went to bed. Today, of course, I smoke cigars. And, touch wood (with my twisted stump of a hand), my teeth are not so bad. One or two have sheared off, but they are stable to the point where they're not getting any worse. The doctor I see has me on a special mouthwash. He told me that if a decayed tooth had a decayed nerve it would be okay. And so far, he's been proved right because I've had a decayed tooth in there since I was a small boy. I know my teeth are not pearly white but, to be honest, I wouldn't care if they were black. As long as I have teeth I can chew with, and they are still in my mouth, that will do me just fine.

So that's my body, and that's what I'm putting up with. And putting up with that and all the constant challenges is why I need my dossy days. But don't think I'm a whinge. I just get on with it, and I have for the last 36 years. I'll tell you how I've managed, but to do that we'll have to go right back to the beginning.

Chapter Two

I WAS born Jonathan Kennedy at Preston Hospital in North Shields in the North East of England on November 4th 1966. I arrived with no skin on my right leg from my knee downwards, just bare flesh open to the elements. I came by caesarean section, because I was faltering in Mother's womb. By all accounts it was a rush job. No one knew what was wrong with me when I arrived, but the hospital read up on my symptoms and diagnosed me as 'junctional'. That meant my skin wouldn't replace itself and, because of the risk of infection, I would probably die very soon after birth. There was no hope. My parents were basically just told to go home, forget about me, and get on with their lives.

Of course, it wasn't as simple as that. Mother wasn't

allowed to see me for the first two days of my life, but she would not forget about me. She *couldn't*. She visited every day, gradually learning how to handle me. There was nothing the hospital could tell her – they didn't know how to handle me themselves. Eventually Mother was able to take me home, although she had to bring me back in the evening because she just couldn't cope on her own. But she never gave up, and soon learnt what to do. In those days there was no help at all. Today there is a charity that employs a specialist nurse to visit parents and hospitals – I'll get on to that shortly – but when I was born there was no support. It was just a case of: 'You want him, you can have him. Just get on with it.'

I was a lot for Mother to handle at the time, not least because my brother Simon was only 22 months old when I was born, and a handful in his own right. But she's an angel that woman. I can't remember much about those days, I'm glad to say, for it must have been hell. They wouldn't even let Mother breast-feed me, so I was weaned on carnation milk. I'm certainly a good advert for that stuff, aren't I?

I've been told that I had a permanent blister down the centre of my tongue that had to be burst every time they wanted to feed me. Apparently, it was so big that at times I couldn't even close my mouth. Then, when I went onto solids, my throat became so sore that I couldn't even swallow my own saliva. It must have been a nightmare for me, for Mother, for everybody. I don't know how I survived it.

Eventually my diagnosis was narrowed down to Dystrophic Epidermolysis Bullosa. Mother and Father had no idea about the condition: how to treat me; what was good; what was bad; what hurt; what didn't. They received no support or financial help. It wasn't until the Joseph Rowntree Foundation – a charitable trust – visited us years later that Mother learnt she'd missed out on claiming an allowance for me, and a carer's allowance for herself. Until then they persevered on their own. It was just a case of trial and error. And, oh boy, what errors there were!

Back then we lived in Seaton Sluice, on the North East coast, where Father heard that salt water toughened the skin. Every night he'd go down to the beach and return with two buckets of seawater to bathe me in. Oow! I still have the memory of that pain. He did this so often that, one day, a curious neighbour asked Father if we were keeping a shark or some strange sea creature in the house. But it was only little old me.

Father also got it into his head that exposing my skin to fresh air would help. One time he stripped off all my bandages and stuck me out in the garden. The flies enjoyed that episode more than I did, I can tell you. I've hated flies ever since.

When I reached 'pram age' people always stopped to ask Mother how I was. Because I was bandaged, strangers always thought I was a battered child. When they found out that it was a 'disease', as they called it, they kept their own children miles away from me in case it was contagious. They didn't want their little darlings catching anything that Jonathan had. I know I sound a little bitter here, and I am. I know it wasn't their fault, and in their shoes I'd probably have done the same. But it was just... I was so lonely as a child.

I was left on my own a lot when I was young. We'd go to places as a family, and Father would say I had to stay in the car while they checked to see if it was safe, that there weren't crowds of people that could squash me. And I'd wait and wait in the back of the car like a pet dog. By the time they got back whatever we'd gone to see would be over. Of course, their excuse was always that it wasn't very good and wasn't worth going to see in the first place. Shit man, it couldn't have been that bad 'cos they were away for ages! Oh boy, the times that happened. I didn't like those situations at all.

A lot of the time I'd be left at home. Sometimes Simon would be there, but other times he would be out with his friends. Mother would be away on her horse, and Father would be out on his bike or out with the dogs. I'd be left to entertain myself. There were lots of times like that. We just couldn't seem to be a family, at least not without me being left out. They all had their pursuits, and they'd always be away for longer than they said they would. I'd be sitting, staring at the clock, waiting. If it wasn't for television, I don't know what I would have done. I'm sure I would have gone mad. It was bad enough having to cope with the condition – being left on my own like that always used to hurt.

I don't know why, but Father could never call me by my true name. To him, for whatever reason, I was 'Moysher' or 'Jacko', anybody but Jonathan. So I called him 'Cato'. It was the first thing that came into my head. I can play that game too! Jonathan actually means 'a gift from God'. Looking at me you'd be made to wonder. Later on I got everyone to call me 'Jonny'.

My parents have learnt a lot through having me as their son. But, on the other hand, I've also deprived them – and Simon – of so much. Simon, who I nicknamed 'Pongo', had a hard time at school because of me. He was always in fights in those days, when kids shouted at him that he had a 'scabby brother'.

Pongo and Cato spent a lot of time together. There was one time I remember when Cato was into this cooking lark and began making curries, and Pongo helped him out. Mother was out, and they called me into the kitchen to test their recipe, offering me a teaspoon with powder on it. Pongo was revelling in it, saying how wonderful it was. At the time we had all been going through a phase of eating

Horlicks from a spoon, and I thought this must be something similar, so I took it. It was a spoonful of curry powder! That was not a good episode. It was terrible. No amount of water could get rid of the burning taste. I don't know whose idea it was, but it was just one of their little games. 'Let's have fun!' I was a thing of amusement to them.

In his own way, Pongo was getting back at me because he couldn't thump me like you would a normal brother. Father just thought it was a big joke. But there were one or two times when it got a bit silly, and it didn't help that I was very gullible. Cato would do this 'hocus-pocus' magic thing with us. He said if I was ever naughty he'd turn me into a frog, and I believed him. Well, one day when Mother was out again, Pongo and Cato were messing around as usual, and I must have been doing something 'naughty'.

'Mind, if you do that, we'll turn you into a frog,' Cato reminded me. I didn't stop whatever it was, so they did the 'hocus-pocus' thing and Cato said, 'Yes, you're a frog now.' And, of course, Pongo agreed. They both insisted that I was a frog, and I believed them, totally. It was only when Mother came back that I was able to ask, 'Mam, am I a frog?' They were so convincing that for a long time afterwards I still thought I was a frog.

As I began to get older I was allowed to stray a bit further from our house. By now we lived in Whitley Bay, further down the North East coast. There was a cemetery nearby, and that basically became my playground. I'd play around the graves and crematorium. A morbid sort of existence, yet I enjoyed it. It was quiet, because no other kids would go there, you see. My parents knew it was reasonably safe and I wouldn't get hurt. Other children would be in a playground, kicking balls and playing on swings and bikes, and I'd be alone in the cemetery. I thought it was good, though. It was laid out with paths and roundabouts, wide enough for a hearse to get around. It became like a mini-highway for me and my little go-kart, and I practically lived in that place.

I did get into some scrapes though, sometimes literally. One time I remember running past the next door neighbour's house, then tripping over and sliding along the ground. I didn't put my hands out to save myself, either. I only have a little nose, but I took the skin right off it, as well as off my lips and chin. It all just hung there. Oh, what a state I was in. There was grit and rubbish and everything in it, too. It was a bad incident that one. I actually slid along on my face.

One of the most annoying habits my parents had when I was younger was wanting to burst my blisters. If I had a blister on my arm or neck they would get their thumb and finger and nip it. Didn't matter where they were, what they were doing, or what time of day it was, they always had time to nip. I don't know if they took pleasure from it —

although they seemed to at the time – but it stung like hell. Some of the blisters were quite big, and they'd seep all over me. The idea behind bursting them was to stop them from spreading. 'Let's get rid of them now!' was the battle cry, instead of going to the hygienic bother of getting scissors and a gauze swab to dab up the mess. 'Jonny's got a blister! Let's nip it!' I mean, they could have had dirt under their fingernails or anything, then my war wounds would go septic. But at least it kept my parents happy. God, the things were painful enough without all that nipping. 'Oh, there's another'. *Nip!* 'Got Jonny again!' I would be left with a wet patch somewhere and a stinging mess, and they would just go off and carry on with whatever they were doing.

As you might imagine, I've spent a lot of time in hospital over the years. My first memory of being there was when I was three or four, when Mother, Father and Simon went to Norway for a holiday. And boy, did they need that holiday – their first ever. I was left in a hospital because no one else could cope with me. I remember wondering why I was there, because nobody was doing anything to me, and my parents didn't visit. I was totally confused, and every day I'd climb onto this chair by the window and stare out, wondering if they were coming back for me. Then, on the day they did come to pick me up, I was so excited, jumping up and down on this chair, that I slipped and skinned my leg. Of course there were tears and mayhem again, because I was in such agony. It was an absolute nightmare. But they brought me back a toy swan and truck with big red wheels. I remember the presents clearly, but I've no idea what happened to them. Funny old world, isn't it?

When I was a boy no one knew how extensive my condition was, so Mother gave me the same meals as everyone else was having. I always remember being the last sat at the table. It wasn't only a case of being a slow eater, either. I just couldn't manage it. I remember one dinner time when it was lovely outside and I wanted to be out in the sunshine. Everybody had finished their meal, but I had minced beef left on my plate. I'd eaten the potato, managed the cabbage and carrots, but there was this mince left. And boy, was I struggling. My pudding was sitting there as well, with evaporated milk to go with it. Pouring evaporated milk on things made them easy to swallow. So what did I do? I went and poured evaporated milk all over the mince. It was foul! How one learns as a child! But it was a slow process, and in those days I had to try and eat what everybody else was eating.

Had we known more about the condition, we might have blended foods a lot sooner and done without others that were harmful, like meat, which I don't eat anymore. I have to be careful about what I eat, but I'd get it wrong when I was younger. 'Oh yes, you can eat all those biscuits, but you can't eat your dinner,' Mother would say. But it's all to do with the texture of the food and what it does in your mouth. Put a lump of meat in your mouth and what will happen? It will sit there until doomsday unless you can chew it. Put a hard biscuit in your mouth and, without even chewing or moving it, the saliva softens it and you can squash it with your tongue. It's very difficult to make people understand that. Mind you, people must reckon I'm tight when I'm out in the pub, because I take up to two to three hours to eat a bag of crisps. I have to eat delicately, you see, so they don't cause traumas in my mouth.

The problem with meat is that I have to chew it and chew it and the trauma on my gums and tongue is such that it's not worth the hassle. And it doesn't digest quickly, so it doesn't help my stomach either. I stick to vegetables now. You can get some great vegetarian sausages too, and I love them. So I'm a vegetarian, but I don't go on about it. I don't care what other people eat. They could eat a steak in front of me and I wouldn't care. I'm only a vegetarian because it suits my stomach and me. I'm not averse to the killing of animals. I used to see that all the time when I lived in the countryside.

I suffered from terrible constipation when I was younger through eating meat, because my digestive tract is so slow. I remember that when I was a boy, life in the evenings seemed to revolve around going to the toilet. I'd just sit and sit. And I'm not one for reading on the toilet, so it was just a case of sitting there and thinking; contemplating. And, through a lot of straining, I'd end up with something the size of an acorn – and be very proud of the fact that I'd even managed that.

I remember a time when I was about four and I'd been in hospital to get some teeth extracted. Just as I was ready to go home a consultant came around my bed with a load of students and found I was constipated. Of course the consultant wasn't just going to leave me to it. 'Let's clean the little chap out,' he decided. I was still on a drip and, by the time Mother arrived to take me home, they had given me an enema through it. Within minutes you could hear my stomach swirling like a washing machine, a bubbly mass of gurgles. Then they took me to the 'sluice room' and sat me on this trolley, but unfortunately they didn't seem to be prepared. All they could come up with for me to use were kidney-shaped cardboard trays. Whether they had a rush on bedpans that day, I'll never know, but they kept pushing these little cardboard trays under me, and I kept merrily filling them up.

Whatever they had given me had made me drowsy, and I didn't really know what was going on. It was all just happening around me, so, thinking that the staff had control of what I was doing, I decided to have a pee. It turned out that neither they nor I had full control of my functions and I ended up soaking two nurses that day. Never mind, it's an occupational hazard for them. They cleaned me out and I went home.

It got to about a week later and I still hadn't been to the toilet, so Mother panicked and took me down to the local hospital – only to learn from them that this was all part of the condition. She thought that once they had emptied me out I'd be normal and they'd be able to get me into a proper routine, but that wasn't possible because I wasn't getting a proper diet. I still wasn't able to digest food, so things were just gonna get blocked up again. Why they bothered in the first place, I'll never know. I had already worked myself into a routine of blocking up, emptying out. They emptied me out without really needing to. But still, I got two nurses, which, when you look back, was me getting my own back.

Chapter Three

WHEN I was an infant I went to Woodlawn School, which was in North Shields. It was a special school for children with physical and medical needs. The school had its own grounds, with loads of space and trees where you could lose yourself, even around the back of the school where you weren't meant to be. This offered a great feeling of freedom for me.

I didn't like many of the teachers there, but Mrs Noon was my worst enemy. She knew she couldn't reprimand me like she did with the other kids. They got slapped on the hand with a ruler, but I couldn't have that and she knew it. So, when I got into trouble, she would walk around the classroom, come up behind me and slap the back of the chair. 'Whey ooh!' She didn't dare touch me, but she couldn't leave it, couldn't just tell me off, she had to get a bit of physical torture in there. She was a living nightmare. Thankfully that only lasted until I moved into Mrs Wiseman's class, but life wasn't exactly a breeze there either.

There was a lad there who made my life a misery by picking on me all the time, and I couldn't understand why. I won't name him, but he was a horrible lad. I took a pack of Top Trumps cards to Mrs Wiseman's class one day and left them on my desk. The next time I looked they were gone, and I knew exactly who had taken them. The following day I went down for the bus and he came over to me and said, 'I had a good game of Trumps last night.' He actually admitted it! I tried everything I could to get them back. I even went to see the Headmaster about it, but I couldn't prove anything. So that was that, and I was so upset. They were just stupid cards, I suppose, but they meant such a lot to me. They were *mine* – not his. That lad was always on the lookout to get me. If he could push me or knock me down, he'd be there and do it. And he wasn't just horrid with me, he was that way with everyone.

About a year later I got a 'gang' together. You know what it's like at school – you have your friends. Anyway, one day we all surrounded him, and he got quite a beating, I can tell you. It was very naughty. At that young age, you know it's not right to hit people, but like it or not, sometimes it's the only language bullies understand. I mean, when you're young and someone is out to get you, you're gonna be out to get them back — and the school weren't doing their bit to help.

He changed a bit after the beating, but I still couldn't forget about him stealing my Top Trumps. One Christmas he came in with a haversack filled with Matchbox cars, all in their boxes; presents from Santa. He was trying to be buddy-buddy. He was always protective of his toys and had me count all his cars, and there was this one motorbike I really liked. So I thought, 'Right, I'm gonna have that.' When the end of the day arrived I hung back in the class-room, grabbed the motorbike, then headed off for the bus with it tucked safely away in my pocket. The next day I saw him get off the bus. 'I enjoyed playing with the bike last night,' I said to him. I did feel a bit uncomfortable about getting my own back. He tried involving the Headmaster to sort it out, but they had no proof. So, he kept my Top Trumps and I kept his Matchbox motorbike.

At school I ran around like the other kids, and I fell down like them, too. But when I fell down it was a major disaster, because I wouldn't just graze my knee, I'd take all the skin off it. I can still picture myself falling towards the ground and thinking, 'Here we go again!' – it happened that often.

There was this one time coming home in winter when Mrs Brown, another teacher, held my hand as she saw me off the bus and into our house. It was a cold day and the ground was covered in a layer of solid ice. Walking was almost impossible as I slipped and slid away from her with each step, clinging on for dear life. And, of course, it's human nature to hold on to anyone who slips in those situations, and Mrs Brown was no exception to that rule. She didn't stop me from skidding though, and down I went, sliding along the ground. Only, I left my hand behind. I totally slid out of my skin, leaving Mrs Brown holding on to what amounted to a human glove. She was so upset that she even thought of giving her job up because of it.

Of course, the saga didn't end there for me. The fun really began when the bandage they put around my hand became knitted together with gunge and hardened so much that it wouldn't come off no matter what was done to it. I ended up in the Fleming Memorial Hospital for sick children in Newcastle for a week while they tried every method under the sun to take it off. That place was worse than the Gestapo Headquarters. Adults wouldn't put up with what us children had to in that evil place. It closed down in the late 80s, thankfully.

Back at school, I found that I could make myself turn white – always a great trick to cause panic at school. 'Jonny's not well! Let's get him away!' I'd just sit for awhile, and when they'd ask if I wanted any lunch I'd whisper meekly that I couldn't, and I'd be all pitiful and terrible. The only thing they could do was phone Mother and get her to pick me up. This practically became a daily event. I often said to Mother, 'Why are you bothering sending me to school? You know I'll be back for lunch.' But she'd send me all the same, then have to come and pick me up. She told them umpteen times that I was putting it on, but I don't think they quite believed her. I bet they were thinking, 'What a wicked mother Jonny has, she obviously doesn't want the hassle of looking after her child and putting up with him. Sending him to school in that condition when he's so obviously ill.' I even told people at school that the family had their main meal of the day at lunchtime, and I was only given jam and bread when I returned from school. Heaven knows what they thought of Mother after that.

I was always looking for ways out of going to school. One day after breakfast I said to Mother, 'Are you sure you should send me?'

'Yep!' came back the sharp reply. It was obviously a thing of principle that I was going to be sent.

'Well,' I said, 'I'll see you later then.' And off I went.

I got into class and, sure enough, as soon as lessons began there I was with my head on the desk moaning.

'Are you OK?' they asked.

'I'm not well.'

'Would you like to lie down?'

'I'll lie down a bit.'

'Can you manage anything?'

'Can't manage a thing.'

'Ring his mother!' they cried.

Mrs Buckingham came to escort me out. I was a few paces in front of her, and how I didn't actually crack up laughing I'll never know. Mother arrived and was walking down the corridor towards us, and I was looking at her, smiling as if to say, 'I told you so.' It beamed across my face. I was literally just about to crack up, while Mrs Buckingham had such a stern look upon her face. She said to Mother, 'Don't you understand that Jonathan is not well? You shouldn't keep sending him to school.' And every time Mrs Buckingham gave me a look I'd give her a woeful one back, then I'd look at Mother with a grin that revealed the truth.

Off we went home, and that was it. It was a skive and a laugh, but it was good because when I got home I had all my own things around me. I had the TV, the dog was there, and if Mother was going shopping it was stimulating to go with her. It was far better than sitting talking to other kids who led as dull a life as I did myself. I mean, we were doing nothing and I know the others would rather have been at home too.

At Woodlawn they were supposed to teach you to read and write and do basic maths, but nobody seemed to give a toss. It was just a case of, 'Get on with it'. As long as we weren't making a fuss we could do anything we wanted — chat for hours, play games, anything! There was no real education. It was very rare that they pushed any work onto you. When I eventually left school I had the reading ability of a seven-year-old, and I was getting on for fifteen! Mother had to teach me at home to get me up to standard. Only when Simon came home from his school, laden with home-work, did I think to myself that, actually, it wasn't so bad that my school has been so easy.

School was an utter waste of my time. It's supposed to have changed now because of the curriculum. It would be interesting to know whether that means the teachers have actually got to do something with their charges now. It's ironic that teachers in a disabled school are paid more than in ordinary schools because they have more to cope with, and yet — in my experience — they do less. Makes you sick, like, doesn't it?

I did learn some things at Woodlawn School, although you couldn't really call it an education in the academic sense of the word. One teacher, Mr Walton, knew that his pupils were not going to have an ordinary working life, so he aimed his teaching towards social skills and politeness: holding doors open; saying please and thank you; eating properly. He must have thought that at least we would be able to survive in the community and be more accepted if we were polite.

When I got to about 11 or 12, everyone at school was talking about a trip to France. I knew this happened every year but, as it was always people from the senior school who went, I thought nothing more about it. Then, one day, Wendy Anderson and I were given letters to take home. No one else in the class got a letter, and I was convinced that it could only mean trouble. What had I done wrong now? I took the letter home fearing the worst, but it turned out to be from the Across Society, which runs trips to Lourdes every year on specially-adapted busses. Wendy and I had been chosen to go. It cost £200 and was run by the 'Little Sisters of the something or other'. It was quite exciting, and before long one of the 'Little Sisters' came to the house to see how Mother did my dressings, and then did them herself while getting accustomed to me. It was fine, she was nice, and I got on well with her. Then came the morning of the trip. Typically, yet again, it turned out to be another nail in the coffin of life.

We had to get up early to drive to Newcastle to catch the bus. It was about four in the morning and we'd only driven a short distance along the road when, all of a sudden, *bedump, bedump*, one flat tyre. We all had to get out of the car, Father couldn't find the jack, and it was freezing cold. Isn't it strange how nothing ever runs how you'd like it or how you plan it? Has anyone ever fathomed that one out? Does anyone know why things don't run smoothly? Anyway, we finally got there, and the bus set off, picking up a few others as we drove down to the ferry on the south coast.

I hadn't realised what the trip was about. I knew this Sister had come to our home quite a bit, but Lourdes wasn't the sort of place I'd heard of, and Lourdes and France just didn't go together in my head. When I was told I'd be going I thought it was just a short trip out, but when we got down to the ferry it dawned on me that we were actually leaving the country and Mother wasn't going to be there. I relied on Mother a lot, so that alarmed me. I have to admit I was homesick, badly homesick – and we hadn't even left the country. I thought, 'I've had enough, just send me home'. The other people on the trip were all strangers, apart from the Sister and Wendy, and I had to sleep on a seat, which wasn't the most comfortable thing. The food wasn't all that good either. And I needed such a lot doing to myself, bandage-wise. I didn't like it at all.

When we arrived in Lourdes, things seemed a little bit better. Maybe it was being cooped up on the coach, but I started to get to know people, and the sun was shining and I thought, 'Well, this is a new experience. This is France. Enjoy it.'

The organisation owned special chalets, which was good. It would have been impossible for us to stay in a hotel, since we all needed so much care and attention. I remember Father giving me a load of sweets to share with the others during the journey, and I kind of neglected to dish them out. I had one of those cagoules with a top pocket, and I had all these sweets crammed in, and I was in a buggy thing that they pushed me around in, so I just sat in it and pigged out.

The chalets had their own priest, and they held Catholic masses every morning. Wendy and I had to go along, but, as neither of us were Catholic, we didn't get involved with the wine and bits of bread, missing out on the goodies. Everyone got *something* for going except us.

We were to be immersed in the water too – the 'miracle water' that's supposed to heal you. The water was in marble baths and was absolutely freezing. I took my clothes off, except for my underpants, and they put me in this latticed stretcher and lowered me down. Well, you know what it's like when you hit cold water. I could hardly get my breath back. The men who were lowering me in took one look at me gasping for breath and quickly pulled me out before the water had even covered my knees. I later heard that someone had a heart attack and died from being plunged into the bitterly cold water. I suppose they'd class that as a miracle, since death is a cure in itself. I considered it a miracle that I *didn't* have a heart attack.

Going into the water had been my biggest fear on the day, so I was pleased to get it out of the way. At night we joined a torchlight procession, which was marvellous. I really enjoyed it. We all had candles with paper shades around the flame to stop them blowing out. I quickly found that if you tipped the candles you could set the shade alight. Guess who had the biggest flame that night. I certainly made sure I stood out from the crowd with my own special lantern. Lourdes hadn't offered any miracles, but I was still young enough to give anything a bash. With good and bad points, at least it was a trip away for a bit.

A couple of years later, the school was visited by the Lions Club, an organisation that helps good causes. They must have had a large amount of funds that they didn't know what to do with. Anyway, they came to the school and said they would give everybody a wish. All we had to do was say what we would really, really like to do. Well, some kids said they would like to go to a sweet factory. I think they had the image of Willy Wonka's Chocolate Factory in mind, not a proper factory where people wearing rubber gloves just chuck sweets into boxes. Still, that is what some kids asked for, and got.

Some of the wishes seemed very basic to me. One kid wanted to visit a police station, and another lad wanted to go on the new local Metro train, which was being tested at the time. A few of us got onboard with that wish and got to drive the train.

Then it came to my wish. But what did I want to do? I had been on the Across Society trip to Lourdes, and had received some of their literature. In it there was a mention of Jimmy Savile – *Jim'll Fix It* himself – either launching a new bus (if that is what you do with a new bus) or going on some outing helping people. So I decided I would like to meet Jimmy Savile, and thank him for all the work he had done for the Across Society.

'Don't be silly,' the Lions Club said. 'Think of something else.'

So off I went and thought about it. I decided I'd quite like to go on an aeroplane. Others had been saying they'd like to go to visit an airport, but I said I would like to go on Concorde. But nothing came of that and, really, I *did* want to meet Jimmy Savile. The way things were going, I thought I wasn't going to get anything out of it at all. Never mind.

Two days later, Mr Walton came into the class with a letter for me to copy out in my handwriting explaining that I wanted to meet Jimmy Savile. I think I had to write it out twice because it wasn't neat enough for them the first time. After it was accepted, a gentleman from the Lions Club came to the house to tell me I would be going down to London to the *Jim'll Fix It* programme, and he invited Simon and Mother, too.

In London we were met at the train station by security and taken straight to the studio, where we were seated on beanbags right at the front of the audience. Then Jimmy Savile came out, and he made quite a fuss of us. It was grand because every time there was a break he would have us over and let us sit in his famous chair and wave to the audience. It was great fun.

Afterwards, we went back to Jimmy's dressing room, had a chat with him, and he introduced us to Angus Ogilvie – the husband of Princess Alexandra – and a few others. When we had to leave, Jimmy got hold of Mother's hand and bent to kiss it, only he didn't kiss it properly, he just wriggled his lips over it. Poor Mother, she didn't know where to put herself! It was a good experience though, and I loved it. So you can see I got a lot out of school – except an education.

While we were in London, Mother decided to take us for lunch at the revolving restaurant in what was then called the Post Office Tower. The meal was absolutely superb. I've never had potato like I had there. It was perfect, and the floor went around and around four times while we ate. At the end of the meal they brought us a tiny cup of coffee. Simon and I thought it must just be a sample, because it came in such a small cup. It was like a doll's tea set. The menu said 'coffee afterwards,' but I think that was stretching it a bit. We looked at each other and thought, 'Oh well, fair enough,' and tossed it down. We couldn't believe that was it. But it was a great experience, and the restaurant closed shortly afterwards, so you can't get up there any more. It really was grand.

Around this time, my best friend Andrew and I would go down to his house during the summer holidays when his mam and dad were out at work. We'd often use their telephone to ring people up – or wind them up, more like. I'd pretend to be working for a company and I'd ring people and say things like, 'Hello, I'm from Storey's Carpets. I have a carpet on my list here that's to be delivered to your house today.'

They'd swear blind that they hadn't ordered a carpet, but I'd insist they had. We'd go on winding them up, and winding them up. I loved it.

We had another one where I'd ring someone using a parrot's voice, and when they answered I'd say, 'Polly's a cracker! Polly's a cracker!'

This would go on for a bit until, eventually, Andrew would take the phone and say, 'Aye, look, I'm terribly sorry but I've been training my parrot to speak. He's quite an intelligent bird and it's a digital phone. He knocks the receiver off and presses some buttons and thinks it's grand because he can hear voices on the other end.'

'Eee! Isn't that wonderful,' they'd say. 'Eee! Can you put me back onto the parrot? George, come and listen to this! There's a parrot on the phone!'

It was so funny. Andrew and I would be cracking up. The Storey's carpet one was the best, though, as people would get so wound up about it. Sometimes we'd ring them back days later, and get them even more annoyed.

'Well, I didn't order a carpet,' they'd say. 'I can tell you.

I *didn't* order a carpet!'

'Well it's down here on my list, pet!'

Wicked, wicked children. See, even in the midst of all that is horrible, I could still have fun.

Chapter Four

L IKE I said before, Dystrophic Epidermolysis Bullosa is what I suffer from, and it's difficult to get your tongue around. Add 'Research Association' on the end and it's even worse, but that's the name of the charity. Dystrophic Epidermolysis Bullosa Research Association, or DebRA for short. Phyllis Hilton formed it in 1978 because she had a daughter called Debra, a sufferer who died when she was in her teens. We heard about DebRA when I was 12 years old, through a woman's magazine Mother was reading. They only met once a year, at their Annual General Meeting, so when that time came around off we went down to Birmingham to check it out.

It was the weirdest thing for me, to actually *see* other sufferers at the AGM, rather than hearing that they existed was a big thing for me. I knew there were others out there, but they had always seemed distant, like 'space people', to me. Now I knew there were others with the same condition – it wasn't just me. Here were people getting together to talk about their fears, things they had tried and stuff like that. It was an odd sensation and I just sat there for ages doing what many, many able-bodied people do to me – I just sat and stared. There was nothing else I could do. It was like discovering a new life-form. I was amazed, bewildered, shocked – with so many emotions running through me, it was impossible to decide what I actually felt.

There were sufferers of all ages, and their parents, too. The parents got a lot out of it, meeting other parents, learning about things they had all tried, things that worked, things that hadn't, the kind of drugs available and their side effects, and the assistance they'd had from doctors. You need this kind of thing when you're out there alone, to know there are others and to have a support network. Then we learned about Attendance Allowance. *Attendance Allowance?* What was that? It turned out that this was a benefit for people who need help with personal care. We hadn't heard about it before, but thanks to Birmingham we found out that Mother was entitled to it as my carer. It was probably relief that I felt at the end of it all – relief that I wasn't the only one on the planet who had EB – not that I'm glad to see others suffer too, but to know you're not alone does help raise your morale a bit. The meeting also gave me a sense that we were beginning to make progress, slowly but surely. We could get help and the charity was active. That was a good start.

DebRA has grown a lot since then. It collects money to aid research, and pays for a nurse and doctor to go around hospitals and homes with help and information – something that was never available when I was a kid. They're not just finding cures for this condition; they're coming up with treatments to do with other conditions too, skin culture to aid those with bad burns, and research into other ailments. I do a lot of stuff to raise funds and awareness with them now, events and activities, and I'm glad to be able to do my bit to help.

Since the Association only meets once a year, most of my communication with the charity is by telephone or letter. I keep in touch with how others are doing, and learn what is new on the market and how the research is coming on to find a cure. But I don't really mix with others with EB. I like to be on my own. I know I look like those that I see – and am probably a lot worse than most – but it depresses me to be constantly reminded. I just want to be with ordinary people and get on with my life, otherwise I'd be pulling myself down by telling myself I can't do this or that, or can't go here or there. It just doesn't seem healthy to me to sit around discussing disabilities, so I don't have friends with

EB, don't have them visit, and don't associate with them at all.

Having said all that, at one of the DebRA AGMs I did make friends with a girl from Stockton called Joannah. We met on the train going down to Birmingham. She'd never seen another sufferer before, and she just stared at me. I knew exactly how she felt. Her parents had just heard about DebRA and were full of questions because this was their first contact with anyone else who was dealing with the condition.

Once we arrived and were having drinks, I lit up a cigar. 'Oh, you can use matches!' she said. 'I can't.' Joannah always burnt her thumb when using matches, so she began fumbling with some cigarettes. 'I use a lighter,' she said, proudly, a smile growing across her face. We ended up showing each other how we each managed.

One school holiday I got a telephone call from the Appeals Director of DebRA. She asked me if I would do her a favour, and I said yes even before I knew what it was. She told me the Royal Air Force had raised some money from a sponsored cycle ride and they would like a sufferer to go and collect the cheque. One of the airmen's wives had given birth to a baby with a 'junctional' condition, and they were curious to see what a living sufferer had to put up with. I thought to myself, 'Fine! No problem!' Then the Appeals Director asked me if I had a passport, because the cheque needed to be picked up in Germany. Show me the way!

We went to the Post Office to arrange for a passport, and the experience of that day really took a lot of coming to terms with. By that time my hands were what some might call *deformed*, although, believe me, I do not like using that word. I'd never thought about it before, but I left the part of the passport application form that asked for 'distinguishing marks' blank. I thought they meant birthmarks or something like that. But then the woman behind the counter looked at me and said, dispassionately, 'Oh yes, of course, deformed hands.' I didn't like hearing that word, and I really could have thumped her. My hands are my hands. I don't think they're deformed. I was quite disgusted when she used that expression. People can be cruel sometimes; they are too keen to label others with a disregard for their feelings.

We flew to Germany from Luton Airport, where some RAF guys pinned me with a yellow tag with an 'X' on it, which I soon learnt meant 'VIP'. I was treated brilliantly on the plane, and I even got myself some cheap brandy courtesy of the Ministry of Defence. It was marvellous. When we arrived, the other passengers had to wait until the VIP disembarked. Everyone's heads were bobbing up and down over their seats trying to see who the special guest was, so I got up slowly and made my way to the exit, as you do. The Captain and crew were there to see me off, there was an escort at the bottom of the gangway, and a chap saluting. It was absolutely fantastic. It was grand to be Very Important for a day. I could have definitely got used to that kind of treatment.

While in Germany, I stayed with a couple called Sheila and Richard in their home, and they gave me one of the best times I've ever had. They showed me around Germany, and we went over to Holland and went up a windmill. Oh, it was grand. We got in with this other family and went to a leisure centre, too. I loved it. I was over there for three days, and on the Saturday afternoon they did the presentation. The cheque was being split between DebRA and a local kindergarten, so there was quite a lot of folk there. I had a speech to read, which was given to me by the charity. There was a party and food, and it was really good, I enjoyed the whole experience.

Throughout the trip, I was totally on my own. Other than staying with Sheila and Richard, I had nobody with me at all, no family, or anyone. Of course, I didn't have as much trouble with my back then as I do now, so that made things easier. But it was an incredible taste of freedom – not just going out for a bit at home or exploring the grounds at school – this was *real* freedom with me in control of what I did and when I did it. It was just grand. I tried all sorts of food and visited new places, and they sent me back with a box of chocs for Mother. Sheila and Richard really looked after me, and were the first to mention I should write a book about my life and the condition, even at that early age. It seemed a million miles away from reality to me, but did get me thinking. Life was bizarre enough without writing it all down.

In August 1980, when I was 13, Mother and Father bought their dream home – a working farmhouse – and we moved from Whitley Bay to Rochester, way up in Northumberland, close to the Scottish border. Well, Rochester is a three street wonder – the main road to Scotland, and two side streets leading nowhere. One garage, one café, and a Post Office that was located in a house until it moved to the café, and then moved to the garage – until the garage closed. You couldn't get more remote.

There were no facilities for me at all up there, so a supply teacher called Val Telfer had to be brought in to teach me at home. I did six hours a week with Val, and during that time I was taken to Byrness School to do art. Byrness is a tiny village a few miles north of Rochester, and the school was a 'first school' so there were only little kiddies there, but it was great. For, once the kids got to know me, they accepted me with ease. There's no complications with kids, is there? It was probably good for them to have me there, too. It got them accustomed to people with disabilities. It was great fun. I was so happy and I have a lot to thank Val for. If I had been left at Woodlawn, I wouldn't have had anything like this and would not have been able to grow as a person intellectually and socially. It was through this that I began to learn, and I was eventually able to go on to college.

I see those kids from Byrness now, all grown up and sitting in the pub. They're going to Polytechnics or Universities, and by gum I feel old. I was sitting with them when they were just tiny tots. They're all doing this and that, while I seem to have stood still. It's nice to see that they've grown as people too, they still remain my friends and still there is no prejudice or look of fear from them.

At Whitley Bay, we always had dogs, and Mindy, our Yorkshire Terrier, was a gem. Then, when we moved to Rochester someone offered Pongo a ferret, so, to keep the peace, I was offered a cat. Only it wasn't allowed into the house – the plan being for it to be a 'farmyard cat'. We visited a friend whose cat had just had a litter to choose a black kitten. But could we catch any of them? In the end we just grabbed the nearest thing we could, and ended up with a tortoiseshell kitty with a half-white face, a big white bib, and pink nose. I can remember exactly what she looked like because she ended up meaning a lot to me. Coming home in the car, she slept between my legs, and I think that cemented our relationship.

I called her Terbie, because my friend Andrew had a cat

called Topsy and I thought the expression 'topsy-turvy' was 'topsy-terbie'! She stayed outside at the farm, but whenever I came out into the yard she'd run across to see me. When she was younger she had this awful habit of running up my leg, over my back and onto my shoulders. That had to be stopped, and quick. I know it's what cats do, and what kids love, but not me. It was not pleasant, not pleasant at all. She was quite a clever cat though, and I only needed to reprimand her once and she'd learn.

Anyway, little by little, she started creeping into the house. You know what it's like, it's a miserable day and everyone feels sorry for her, so we started letting her into the kitchen. Eventually, she became my shadow. Wherever I was, she'd be there. If I was lying on the settee at night watching telly, she would lie 'washing' my hair. She'd lie there for hours licking and cleaning me as if I was her baby. She knew when it was bedtime, because she was put outside. But she learnt this trick – as soon as the door was closed on her she'd be off around the corner and up onto the hen-house roof. One leap and she'd be onto the gutter of the house and along to my bedroom, where she'd be in through the window and snuggled up to me within seconds. It was grand. In the summer I just left the window open and she'd come and go as she pleased.

Terbie was a fine cat. She had three litters on an electric blanket in the drawer by the side of my bed. It was grand having her as a pet, and as a friend. Just like with the kids at Byrness School, animals don't carry any malice around with them and Terbie was a great friend and companion – no issues, no funny looks, no staring – just accepting and loving. She was still there when I went to college and, boy, did I miss her and I'm sure she missed me. It was difficult to be parted from her like that, because we had such a close bond and had spent every day together up until then. When I returned home, she just didn't seem right. She was lethargic and really unhappy. There had been a few cats in the village that had been found poisoned. I'm not sure if that's what happened or not but, whatever, one day Terbie just slipped away. It really upset me. I thought, 'God! The only thing in my life.' I mean, literally, she was all I had. I had never had a pet before. I'd never had something so special to me. I really missed her.

People have asked why I don't get another cat, but Terbie meant so much to me, and I just couldn't do that. If I ever thought about suicide it was when Terbie died. I felt that I'd had everything taken away from me and there was no point to it all, that there was no fairness in life. Losing Terbie meant losing a soul mate, losing a part of me. With not having her with me, I could hardly see the point in going on. We shared our lives, and without her there didn't seem to be much life left.

Chapter Five

THAT'S my school days over with, and we have come some way together. By now I am sure you realise I have quite some spirit in me. I don't lie down. I don't take prisoners. And since we have come such a way together, I think you will be able to handle the rest of my little old story. The sores! The bandaging! The yuk, basically! And now we're gonna get on to the odour! Anyway, here goes...

At any given time my body is up to 80 percent covered in sores, all in various stages of repair. If I were to let the air get to them I'd have a scab covering me like a suit of armour. I'd be locked in it and unable to move for fear of the trauma it would cause. So I have to keep my wounds covered up with swabs and bandages. A dry gauze swab is rough like sandpaper on an open wound, and it itches like billy-o for a few days until enough puss is created to form a barrier. The puss seals around the swab and bandage, too, so bacteria can't get to it.

When I was younger, I was told to change my bandages regularly. If puss was showing through the bandages they were seen as 'dirty'. But changing bandages is hell for me. For years I had my bandages changed every day, even though I instinctively knew that it was wrong to change them so often. If you keep disturbing a sore you are not giving it a chance to heal and the antibodies within the puss (which the professionals call 'soup' and I call 'gunge') a chance to protect and heal it.

So now I don't change my bandages every day. I only change them when I feel it's necessary. That means summers aren't much fun. There is an odour from the gunge that gets worse in the summer that probably has something to do with sweating. My body has been so completely covered with sores that my sweat glands have been damaged, so that I don't sweat normally from, say, the armpits. The main areas I sweat from are my head and, probably, my backside (the cheeks, you know). If you're sitting for a long time in a wheelchair, you can really sweat. You have bandages on and they're causing pressure, and the body is saying, 'Oh, that hurts. Let's get more protection down there.' It's like relearning biology all the time, getting to know how my body works and how it reacts in different situations and under different medication.

Winter is better for me, because I don't seem to get the odour from the gunge quite as much. But I am very self-conscious of the smell, I think, more than the average person, because they don't know what they're smelling when they get close to me. It's such a different smell. It's not a 'dirty' smell. They can't work out what it is but, if I am in close proximity for too long, they soon work out where it's coming from. I'm very aware of that. That's why I use sprays now. I don't wear aftershave because most of them contain alcohol and it would cause pain and trauma, but I do use toilet water which I spray on my clothes. It helps disguise the smell as the week gets on. I call it 'splash.' I say to Mother, 'Put some splash on, Mother. A quick che, che!' It does help.

I haven't bathed since 1985, and I only bathed before then because it was what you did. It was what the hospitals taught us. It's hygienic and it's what everybody else does. But I have such dry skin that if I stood on cardboard all day there would be, I'm not necessarily saying big flakes, but dust there. Snakes shed their skin and that's what I do, as Mrs Brown found out when she ended up with that human glove in her hand. My skin does it constantly. It's keeping me clean. I mean, I wash my hands and face, but other areas I don't touch with water unless it's really necessary because it softens the sores. Plus you don't know what's in tap water today that could damage my skin. If you watch TV adverts, everybody wants soft skin. I want them to bring out a soap that says, 'This will make your skin like leather!' That would be great, and I'd be the first in the queue to buy it. I don't want to soften my skin, so I just wash my face with water. I do cleanse it. I have moisturisers and those things, but I don't use them a lot because even they are sticky and can irritate. I've learnt to just let nature take its course. Or is that *curse*?

I'm not bandaged all over all the time; only where there are sores. It's mainly the vulnerable parts, like my feet, knees and arms that I use all the time, leaning on them. This means they're prone to blisters, which cause sores. As I get one part healed, another part is coming up. When I go away on holiday I've sometimes put bandages on even if there is no sore there, knowing that if I get knocked I'm going to be in a position where I won't have to worry about it, I'm one step ahead. It can be a bit clarty. But it can be even clartier if I find myself in the middle of an airport and the bandages are either in the luggage or going through customs and I can't get to them, meaning I'm gonna have to wait until the other end to do something about it. I've got to be that step ahead of the game and be prepared.

When my bandages need changing I don't get much advance notice. The gunge seeping through the swab turns it hard as soon as the air hits it, and the swab moulds itself to my body. When the swab hardens it no longer bends, so has a tendency to pop off. This can cause embarrassing situations. If you're in a café, or somewhere there are a lot of people, and you have a manky old bandage drop down your leg, what do you do? 'That's not mine'? I mean, you sort of move your feet as far away from it as possible with a look that says, 'Who's done that?' And hope that does the trick. I tape the swabs on now, so if I feel they're coming off I at least have a chance to get somewhere and see to it. Those are times when you just want to be swallowed up and die.

Everybody out here in the country understands because they know the condition. But it's a very embarrassing situation all the same. You want to deny it happened. They don't want to pick it up. Everybody just stands there hoping this thing will disappear so they can carry on. But can you imagine it happening in a restaurant? I mean, it can't do anything for goulash when a bandage drops down a person's leg. And what are you meant to do with it when you manage to pick it up? Stick it in your pocket? Gunge! You put this grungy piece of material seeping puss in your pocket? Not a good idea. *Not* a good idea at all. Once I was sitting on a barstool in a pub and I pulled myself back and accidentally loosened a swab, which slid down my leg and onto the floor. I picked up the swab, but the only pocket I could hide it in was my jacket pocket containing my money, so I had to remove it every time I needed to buy a drink. Not the best drinking session I've had, I can tell you. It has taken a long time to get over that episode, but now I am over it, and always bandage my legs entirely.

While we're on the subject, there are other things that can be annoying. Like when you go to a restaurant with company who don't know you that well, and you reach for something and a large lump of skin comes out of your sleeve and falls onto the table. This *can* happen! Now, if it's near the edge of the table, you can carry on with the conversation and subtly flick it off. But what if it lands in the middle of the table? What do you do? Some bits can be as big as a thumb! People just don't realise how embarrassing my life can be. Sometimes, it's not good.

These days, my whole back is bandaged from my shoulders down to my coccyx. As the gunge comes through the bandage, it hits the air, dries and turns into a hard crust. So it's a bit like wearing a corset that isn't tied on. Only, every time I move I'm pulling away bits of skin that have stuck to it. If I lie on my side for too long, like when I'm sleeping, the gunge in the middle of the 'corset' goes cold. Then, when I lie flat again, it feels very much like lying on cold custard. And if there is a gap between my shoulder bandage and my neck bandage, the gunge from my back can come around my shoulder and squirt out of the crack all over the side of my face. I have to sit up and put the light on, clean myself up, get myself back to normal, cover the crack up between the two bandages, and go back to sleep. Or try to. And there will be air bubbles trapped between the flesh and the bandages that keep popping as I move. I try so hard to stay still, but I'm creaking and groaning. All night there are bits of stuff happening to me, and I have to live with that all the time. And boy, it's annoying when it's right next to my ear. I've got this gurgle, gurgling all night long. Or, as I say, I roll over, then get a face full of gunge. There have been times when I haven't noticed, and I've woken up with this big dry patch of gunge down the side of my cheek or down my neck. Marvellous! Marvellous fun... I don't think! It's green, too. Yes, green gunge. I don't know why it's green. Green is not my favourite colour. It's certainly not the colour I would have chosen. I mean, people say green is calming. But not this green.

I can't do my back on my own. I can't reach to get the top of the bandage off. I have to get somebody to hold my shoulders on each side so I can peel it off from the bottom like a plaster. I did do it on my own when I was at college, and I still to this day wonder how I managed. I have a vest that is cut down the middle and fastens with Velcro. I lay the vest out on the bed, place my dressings on it, then lie down slowly and stay there for half an hour or so until I know it's stuck. The back is just the worst place, because your arms just don't reach everywhere, especially mine, having been pulled in by the condition. I've seen Mother get in a right state when she's helped with my back, where there have been bits of new skin that have interweaved with the bandage so, as you pull the bandage off, the skin just comes away. Now *that's* the worst, as Mother has to go in with scissors and snip it off, and I end up losing a lot of blood. I try to not let that happen, but it's out of my hands really. That's the only time there is any blood – when I'm taking the bandages off. They are the hell days, and I get a lot of them. I can't wet the bandage to help either. It must stay dry and be taken off dry. *Cracked open* would be a more appropriate phrase. Then the gunge is wiped away, making sure a thin film of the stuff is remaining, gauze swabs are put on and I'm re-bandaged.

It took a lot of years of trial and error before we found the best way of dealing with the condition. Before I went to college I used to have a regular bath to steep myself and allow the bandages to come off by themselves. But changing them all at once is heavy going. It takes quite a bit out of me having so much discomfort. If I change one at a time at least I know where the discomfort is gonna be, and I can concentrate on that area and try and get over it quickly. Psyche myself up.

Obviously this is extremely painful, and I can swear a *lot*. I know that affects Mother. I try not to upset her, but she sees how much pain I'm in and it does distress her. She never shows it though, not in front of me. I've heard from Father that I should try harder, and that sort of thing, but when you are in such agony, shouting and swearing is all you can do to help to relieve the pain. It's getting it out. Mother is there, but she's helpless. She feels for me because she can't do anything about it and it just... everything just multiplies.

I have tried to do the bandaging on my own. I would try to get the bandages off my back in the bedroom, and Mother would sit downstairs in the living room with the telly on, loud. But I found it wasn't working. I'd only end up calling her to the bedroom. I still do try and do some bits by myself, but since the condition is screwing me into a ball there are parts I can't physically get to anymore. I have to admit that as I'm getting older there is a diminishing of mobility. Sometimes I need six pairs of hands, especially when... well... when I've got my bottom to do! I try to hold a new swab on, then pull my underpants up, but I can't reach around to my backside when I'm bending, so the swab drops off. I get myself into a right panic. 'Bloody thing!' I'll say, grunting and swearing at it. It would be a comedy, if it wasn't so sad.

As I said at the beginning, today is a 'dossy day'. That's me stuck inside today, drinking, smoking and loving it. Napoleon Brandy is just so good. 'Mmm, yeah!' You can't beat a good brandy and a good cigar. It's still miserable outside, too, but that doesn't really matter. Dossy days are for in here anyway, enclosed in my own safe little world. So what are 'dossy days'?

As I am sure you know by now, my life is just one long bundle of fun. Alright, no it isn't. My life is filled with pain, puss, bandaging, blood loss, more pain, more puss and more bandaging. So I need to have some kind of routine, some kind of system so I can plan, so I can do things. A 'dossy day' is part of this routine and I'd go mad if I didn't have them.

All being well, the routine I live by is a five-day rota. It's not set in stone, and I can change it, but usually the rota goes like this:

Day One: that's back day, when Mother comes over to give me a hand changing my difficult bandages. I don't go out on Day One, because having my back done, cleaned up and re-bandaged takes most of the day to accomplish and to recover from.

Day Two: I'm covered in new bandages and am raring to go. As yet, very little puss has formed, so there is no smell. But, because there is no puss, the itching is absolute hell. That's Day Two. I can go out in the town in my motorised 'popemobile', get about and move around. I hate to lose a moment. I want to be out there. I hate it when my back is fine and I'm stuck here seeing no one. I'm still itching but as the puss spreads it gets less.

Day Three: I'm still out and about. I'm not itching so much, but the smell is there now.

Day Four: It's much the same as Day Three, only the smell is stronger.

Day Five: This is my 'dossy day'. The day before I get my back done. Of course, the smell is even stronger today, but I stay at home. Back day is hell on earth. I need a 'dossy day' to psyche myself up, to prepare myself for back day. That's where the brandy comes in. If I get drunk or merry today, the alcohol will still be in my system tomorrow and will make things less hellish for me. 'Hallelujah for alcohol,' is all I can say.

This might sound strange, but I have come to terms with the condition. I can handle it. But I know I'm deteriorating. As I got older I thought I'd be able to take more responsibility and do it all myself and not rely on Mother so much. But it's turning out the other way round. I need her more now, and there are times I feel a burden to her, but I can't see a way out of it.

Father was never able to bandage me. He just couldn't handle me being in pain, or anyone being hurt. He couldn't deal with things like that. Having said he never did my dressings, there was one time I remember when we were younger that he did take Pongo and I to London on his own. Even then, I was dumped in the hotel room while he and Pongo went off exploring the city. All I got was a rundown of where they'd been when they got back. I did manage to visit some places, but I spent most of the weekend in the hotel while they were out doing the old father and son thing.

Anyway, Father took it upon himself to bathe us while we were in London. It was the deepest bath I'd ever seen, and we used paper cups as snorkels. I don't know how it happened or how he coped, but he must have changed my bandages then. That's the only time I can remember when Father ever did anything like that. Other times when I would do my back or other dressings, he would go out. Or if he was in the vicinity and could hear me crying or swearing, he would start singing or shouting, whistling even. Anything to make it seem like it wasn't happening. He just couldn't handle it. He would never take the pressure off Mother.

I couldn't say, 'Look Cato, Mother has had enough. Give me a hand. I need to have such-and-such done.' It just couldn't happen. Just *couldn't* happen. Even for simple things like meals I always ended up asking Mother. Asking Father to do anything would be a major operation, which would cause more fuss than if I had just asked Mother in the first place. As an example: if I asked him to butter a piece of bread for me, it would be, 'Is this the right bread? Is that enough butter? Do you want any more? Do you want the crust off?' instead of just doing it and letting me say what I needed. If we were having puddings, he'd ask

Mother, right in front of me, if I wanted any. And she'd reply, 'Well ask him. He's sitting right next to you.' And so it goes on. You'd think he had just come into the situation and was new to it. I really felt for him. But sometimes Father was more of a problem to me than my condition.

Chapter Six

NOT long after I left school, we all noticed a change in Granny. She was beginning to become very forgetful, and we knew she'd soon have to come and live with us in Rochester. Mother decided we should all take a holiday while we could, and Paris would be the ideal place. There was Granny, Uncle Denys, Mother, Father and myself. I think Pongo stayed home to look after the farm.

We flew over, settled into a little hotel and began the sight-seeing – the Eiffel Tower, Notre Dame and places like that. One day while we were out the weather turned nasty. It rained steadily and didn't look like it was going to change, so we decided to head for the Louvre. Only, when we got there the queues were huge. I was in my wheelchair, so Cato and Mother decided they would go and ask if I could wait inside, out of the rain, while they returned to the queue. The staff happily agreed, as long as I was out of their way. So I was left in a sort of cloakroom, across from the huge entrance lobby. And I was quite happy with that, because it was a bit warmer in there.

So there I sat for quite a while. My cap was wet and I took it off, not thinking, and put it on my knee. I sat drip-drying, just minding my own business. Then this couple came across, hung their umbrellas and waterproofs up, turned to me and put money in my cap. I looked at the money in surprise, then back at them, and said, 'No, no, no!' and tried to give it back. They just shook their heads and walked away. I was lost for words and turned to the security guard nearby, who gave me such a look. I mean, I didn't ask for it. So anyway, I put the money in my pocket and didn't think anything more about it.

Then it happened again. So I put that money away and put the cap back on my head. I didn't want any more of that. The guards were probably thinking it was just a sly way of having somewhere posh to beg. I thought I'd never see Mother or Father again at this rate, that I'd end up being put away. But they soon arrived, and when I told them about it they thought it was a big laugh. What can a fella do?

We forgot about it and went around the Louvre. It was

smashing, such a grand building. There were some really nice bits of art and things, but I was not impressed with the Mona Lisa. I cannot understand the fuss they make over her at all. It's a little piddley painting behind glass with security guards on either side of it. I thought, 'What a faff!' No way was it bigger than two feet square. It wasn't much of a painting at all.

The next day the sun was shining and we all decided to go somewhere nice for lunch. Cato was pushing me and we ended up way ahead of the others, so he parked me outside a restaurant and went back for them. I thought I was well dressed. I had my jacket on and a tie. I was sitting there quite happily, when this little old French lady wearing a long skirt, shawl and flat hat comes along and puts money on my leg. I didn't even have the cap off this time! From the look of her I was sure I must be better off than she was, but she just put the money on my knee and walked off. There was no trying to give it back to her, either. I thought, 'What am I? Who are these people?' It was a bit over the top.

There was one night when us men went out together – I was in the wheelchair, Cato was pushing and Denys was on the other side – and I got my eye on this lass standing in a doorway. Of course, she was a 'lady of the night'. She had this weird poodle with her that had a really queer expression. Its eyes were just staring – I didn't dare think what it had seen or been through in its life. I caught her eye and made gestures towards Denys (unknown to Denys, of course), and she came hurrying out and tried to get him into her brothel. That was most amusing.

Another time, we found a grand place to eat off the tourist track where I tried frogs' legs, which tasted just like skinny chicken. But when we came out of there, this bull-mastiff dog came over intent on making mischief. It belonged to someone in the restaurant, and would it leave me alone? Would it hell. Cato had to tip me up and wheel me out and down the road to try to escape, but it still followed in the hope of having me for dinner. I smell of raw meat, you see. I probably smelt like a butcher's cart to this dog, and he just wanted some of it. He thought it was great fun, but it was frightening for me. I've had that happen before – a friend's dog is the same. It's a Rhodesian Ridgeback and it wears a muzzle a bit like Hannibal Lecter's mask. It'd press its nose right against me and put its tongue over its nose, drooling. 'Brrr!' Doesn't bear thinking about.

Near the end of the holiday, after my success at getting money off total strangers, Father convinced me that we should do this begging thing professionally. He decided we'd go to the Metro early in the morning and he would leave me there. I was in my chair, and Cato placed me at the top of the steps leading down to the platform, out of view of the ticket office. There were many down-and-outs around Paris, on the underground or sitting on the streets, and I was a bit embarrassed about being given money, 'cos I didn't want to be classed as one of them.

I could see the other scroungers at the bottom of the stairs below me. Some had signs made from bits of board, and there was a woman with her 'sick' kiddie lying across her knee. Well, I knew she was bogus because I had seen her the day before and the kiddie was perfectly fine. I thought 'What a load of rubbish.' So I didn't feel guilty about what I was doing at all. A Metro pulled in and some of the others had their heads bowed looking really sorry for themselves, and I saw some of them getting bits and pieces. I was at the top of the stairs, cap on knee, and people started putting money into it. And there I was, as happy as Larry, a big smile on my face, saying, 'Merci! Merci!' Thumbs up. Well, what passes for a thumb for me.

I thought it was great, but if Mum and Dad didn't hurry up I was sure I'd get mugged since I was doing better than the other scroungers were. Passengers must get sick of seeing crummy, knackered people. And here I was with a smile on my face, being polite. It must have been a change for them. A couple of Metros went by and I was looking in my cap to see what I'd got. I had a few francs by this time, so I put those away and just left the little tiddlers there. I thought, 'I've got this sussed! I can make a living out of this!'

Another Metro came in and I saw the others getting

coppers and I'm waiting at the top of the stairs. 'Merci! *Merci!*' Getting more dosh. I couldn't believe it. It paid for all my duty free that year. I got all my cigars, and I mean I *really did* get all my cigars. I stocked up very well. It was grand. It's good to know that if things get tough I can always nip over to Paris and make a few quid.

Believe it or not, something similar happened again after we got home. Mother and I were shopping at Tesco when this woman came over to me.

'Hello!' she said.

Well, I am always meeting people who know me but who I forget, and I apologise now if I have ever done that to you. I meet so many people and I am really bad with names and faces. I try not to, because it's such a discourtesy. But what can a fella do?

Anyway, she said, 'Hello!'

I said, 'Hello,' back.

She said, 'How are you?'

I said, 'Oh, fine.' I mean, you don't want to go into details do you?

She said, 'I want you to have this,' and she stuffed this bit of paper in my hand.

I said, 'Alright.'

I didn't dare look at it while she was there. Then she just walked away. I looked down and thought, 'What is this?' It was a five pound note. I didn't know this woman from Adam, and have never seen her since. She just walked up to me and gave me a fiver, then walked off. It wasn't even a donation to DebRA or anything. Crazy! I mean, in the middle of a supermarket! It was very strange, but hey if people want to come up and give me money I'm not exactly gonna tell them to bugger off, am I?

Chapter Seven

I HAVE to admit, I was not keen on going to college, but I had a careers officer who said it was something I should try. I couldn't understand it myself. No matter how many exam passes I'd manage, they still wouldn't get me a job. It was way down in Coventry, too, being the nearest establishment purpose-built for the disabled. But I suppose it was an experience, and filled in a year.

It was the first time I'd been away from home for any length of time, and I didn't enjoy the distance. There would be no chance of nipping home if anything went wrong. That in itself was a shock to my system. I'm paranoid about other people doing my dressings and things. They don't know what they're doing, starting from scratch. They go by the book or are in a rush, and need to relearn how to do it for my needs, not by what they think they know. To do them properly you've got to take your time, and you've got to have plenty of it. It's no good rushing in and as I say, I've got to be psyched up for it. I can't be put under pressure, because that's when trouble starts. Mother knows all these things, but at college no one had seen the condition or knew how to care for me. I was just dropped there and had to get on with it myself. I did have help with some of the dressings, but it was very rare and they weren't pleasant experiences.

My not bathing thing all started at college, really. I just didn't have time for such things, because I had so much to do. To take all the dressings off and put them on myself would have taken a whole day, and no way could I take a day out to do something like that. There was a sink in my room, so I got into the habit of having a 'birdbath'. I'd change the bandages on my feet one day, and if I had a bit of time I'd do a knee the next, and so on until it had all been changed. Then I'd start again, bit by bit until each had been replaced and then go back through it all again.

I remember a six-monthly report that was sent to Mother. There was a comment from the matron, saying how nice it would be to see me with my light out before midnight. But I just couldn't do it. I had homework to do, and I had to sort out my bandages, and I also had to supplement my diet.

Even though the people at the college were prepared to give me a diet I could cope with, they never gave me the time to eat it. They had a set time, and I'm a slow eater. Wouldn't you be, too, if your mouth was tiny like mine? I needed an hour, possibly more, to eat a full meal – and that's going at it almost non-stop. Unfortunately, meal times didn't work for me because the bell to return to lectures would go long before I'd be finished. I missed out on a lot of food and nourishment, so when the day was finished I'd get myself off to the shops and buy extra soups and things to make in my room, or I'd get some bread and butter or milk from the canteen. I'd have those to eat, and then I had to get on with my homework, before I could even start changing dressings. There was no way I could have fitted it all in and be in bed by midnight. It was impossible.

College was heavy going, I can tell you. *Very* heavy going, and it took a lot out of me. There were helpers, but they had other people to look after so couldn't give me the time I needed. Consequently, a lot of it I had to do myself. I did get a lot out of college though. It was worth going, because I did learn a lot.

We were the most severely disabled folk they'd ever had at the college. And with the course being a new one, we were making it up as we were going along. There were only five or six of us, and the course concentrated on our interests. Well, I was interested in the theatre, so they asked me if I would like to be a critic. It was great. They paid for me to go the theatre, which was grand. As long as I came back and put a few words down on the computer, they were happy. I saw some great shows – all for free. It was marvellous. I was lapping it up.

There was another person on the course who liked cooking and food, so we went out and sampled restaurants. A lot of the others hadn't experienced going to shops or restaurants, theatres or cinemas, so those experiences were incorporated into the course. I'd done all those things before, but I wasn't gonna miss the opportunity of doing it all again. We ate at Italian, French and Chinese restaurants and the college paid for it all.

I made some friends, but there were also some people who resented me. I didn't do anything to them. Maybe it's the vibes I give out. One day at college I went to collect my mail from the wall docket. There was a letter for me, but someone had burnt a cigarette hole right through the middle of it. That really upset me, because the letter was from Mother. Even though I rang home every night, Mother would still write me letters. It upset me to think that someone would invade my property and do something like that. I took the letter to the Principal, and he thought it was terrible, too. There could have been important documents, or anything, in it. It was going a bit far doing something like that. I knew who it was, and it made me think back to Woodlawn School and to that lad when I was younger. Perhaps these people just can't handle me. I don't know.

As part of the course, we had to get out into the community. We'd been to restaurants, drank wine, visited the theatre and generally made merry. Then it was decided it was important for us to experience another culture, to give us an idea how the rest of the world behaved. It was decided that we'd visit another country. We wrote to various companies for sponsorship and they came up with the money, bless them.

Then someone suggested Venice as a place to visit. And whoever it was certainly set us a challenge. I don't suppose Venetians had seen many wheelchairs. It's just not the place to have them. I don't know what the disabled actually do in Venice, but they don't go around in wheelchairs. There were at least five steps either side of every bridge on every canal, and we were all in our chairs. Anyway, we flew there with five lecturers and two carers, due to the physical work of pulling the wheelchairs across all those bridges. We all learnt a bit of Italian, and it was a marvellous experience. We toured about and saw Canalettos and Tintorettos. We went to all the cathedrals and churches and really experienced Venice. We were treated wonderfully, too.

We dined in yet more restaurants, and with there being a few of us we always sat together at a long table where we'd eat and drink wine. There was one place that had a jazz trumpeter who played Dave Brubeck's *Take Five*, and that really got to me and set the ambience for the whole of that evening. Then, as the night wore on and people drifted away, the owner locked up, put more wine on the table and told us, in Italian, to take our time. We just sat there, mellowed out, and drank the wine. Feeling more relaxed than we had for some time, we all got talking and some of us broke down into tears. It got heavy. Why were we all like this? Why should this happen to us? And that was just the lecturers! We all really got into it. It was just marvellous.

The trip only lasted a week, and was in the spring. That's the time to go to Venice. I mean, everybody says that Venice smells and is dirty, and maybe it is after the tourists have been, but if you go before the tourists get there, it's beautiful. It's a city that just hums with music. I keep telling myself I should go back, but the other half of me says I should never return because it might spoil the memory of it. But I'd like to take people there. Experiencing Venice is a bit like being given cream for the first time. Isn't it exquisite? Isn't it just! Mmm!

On the last day there we were getting ready to go home, and the others were all having their croissants and things, but I just didn't feel like breakfast. I wanted to make every minute in Venice last for as long as I could. How you make a minute last for any longer than sixty seconds I don't know, but I wanted to try. I wanted to experience it all, so out I went and hit the streets of Venice. I had my white cap on, a silk scarf and blouson jacket, which was the fashion at that time. I just strolled out and felt like a million dollars. I mean, I really did feel good. When I say 'strolled out', you'll appreciate it was more of a hobble, really. But it felt like a stroll and I was on my own and lapping it up.

I decided, what better way to finish off the holiday than to give the ladies of our group, plus the daughter of the hotel owner, a red rose each? I'm not usually one for being soppy, or then again maybe I am. I couldn't help it in such an inspiring place. I went up to a florist with my little phrase book and my smattering of Italian and got them all a red rose, each beautifully individually wrapped. I was walking back with them, carrying them properly like the Italians do – heads down, stalks up – when a couple of locals walked past singing. They nodded towards me, and I gave them a 'Ciao!' in return. It was just the business. It really was. If I ever need a memory to make me feel good about Venice, that was it for me.

I took the roses back to the hotel, gave them all out, then hit the streets again. I wanted to be back out there. I had some money left and I wanted to spend it. I bought boxes of sweets, any old rubbish. It didn't matter. It was just to get out there, to feel part of it all. It was fantastic.

While at college I was the Student Union Secretary. Sounds grand, eh? In some respects, though, it was a bit of a waste of time. Basically, no one else wanted to do it. I never thought I'd end up being a secretary. I always thought the skirt and heels would be a bit too awkward.

It was up to me to ring up and book discos and that sort of thing – kind of an events organiser. There wasn't much to do, really. I'd book DJs for Friday nights from a list I'd been given, and I don't think we had a single night when one of them turned up on time or came to the right place. They never seemed to be very interested. We had to start quite early to give everybody a bit of time, because they couldn't stay out too long, bearing in mind that when the disco ended and everyone got home they all needed help to get out of wheelchairs, get undressed and into bed. I had to give a bit of thought to the parents and carers, so it had to stop at around midnight. We never got to have an all night rave-up. Never mind.

The DJs would – with a bit of luck – arrive around ten-thirty and I'd show them where to set up. They'd only bring half their equipment in, their decks and a few lights, never really making any effort. It was the same old routine every time – going through the motions with as little work as possible to fulfil their job description of 'playing records', acting like it was a chore for them to be there. With it being a Friday night, there was no one in the building with any real authority, so when it came to paying them nobody had the courage to complain about their behaviour. So we just had to put up with it. I'd hand over the cheque and they'd go away almost laughing. I'm sure they had a good chuckle once they were on their way home. I really didn't like that. It was total exploitation of the disabled.

After seeing what the DJs did and what equipment they used, and after realising it wasn't a very strenuous thing to do, I thought I'd like to give it a go myself. It couldn't be too difficult to play a few records, and no one could ever make out what they were saying anyway. I was coming to the end of my course and I had the option to stay on and do another year or two if I wanted. But it had been such a strain on me, and I really wasn't happy. Physically, I didn't think I could cope with another year, and I knew there was no way my parents would let me come home and just sit and do nothing. Doing discos would be a way out of that dilemma because I'd have given college up, but started my own business back home instead. You can't say fairer than that, can you? I had a bit of money saved from birthdays, and had pieces of equipment lying around, so it seemed possible. I put the idea to my parents, they agreed, and so I left college and eventually got it set up and running.

It was all done through word of mouth. I wasn't sure how long it would last – I just went with it. But I started getting regular bookings and it turned out to be great! All those late nights – I loved them, even though there were times when I wasn't feeling too good. But I wasn't on my own. My parents gave me a hand setting it up, and there

Me as a bonny baby, and with Father and Simon

My brother Simon and I

Mother, Simon and I in Edinburgh,
Mother supervising my first driving lesson

Clowning around — happy times!

Me in my beloved go-kart,
and riding Mother's beloved horse

God save the Queen at the Silver Jubilee!

A trip of a lifetime on Concorde

Bedroom antics (great posters!),
and getting some fresh air

Catching some sunshine, and having fun at Alnwick fair,
and me with Terbie, the best cat a guy could wish for!

Me in New York City before my trip on the QE2

Meeting Petula Clark on board the QE2, and
visiting the Disney World Magic Kingdom in Florida

Me motoring around, and
surviving a parachute jump

Tackling an assault course for DebRA,
then tackling Sir Henry Cooper!

Meeting Simon Weston and Anthea Turner at a DebRA event

With Nell McAndrew at DebRA's 25th Anniversary do (courtesy DebRA)

DebRA is the national charity working on behalf of people affected by EB (Epidermolysis Bullosa) – a rare genetic condition which causes the skin to blister and shear at the slightest friction, or even spontaneously. There are currently at least 5,000 people living with this devastating condition in the UK. For further information on DebRA, please telephone 01344 771961 or visit our website www.debra.org.uk. Registered charity number: 1084958.

Relaxing with a smoke, and with
Nell at my housewarming party

was a local lad who'd always help out and take over when I got tired. It was so much fun and it did me a power of good. I'd never been able to go to discos, because they were too dangerous for me, but now that I was running them it was another story. I could be there and be part of it and love it because it was mine... and I could have a bit of a bop and a boogie on the stage at the same time and know I wouldn't get knocked by anyone on the dance floor. It was smashing.

I took the disco to all sorts of events – things I would never have been invited to otherwise: wedding receptions, 18th birthday bashes, 21sts, and lots more. I became a people watcher, learning and experiencing more of life from behind my decks than I had ever done before. I always made sure to play my signature tune – *Don't Stop Me Now* by Queen. I love that record, it kind of sums up my attitude to life, especially the line about being like a tiger defying the laws of gravity. The tiger has become a sort of symbol for me, like a symbol of strength.

I did the disco for quite a while, but in the end it got too much for my parents, having to drive me around. They were late nights – and without being rude – the days of them wanting to be up late dancing were long gone. I kept it up for a while after they ducked out, but I knew it had to come to an end. I felt I'd got a lot out of it, and it came to a natural end. Importantly, it had given me something that a normal teenager would have experienced. I had missed out on a lot of things in life and this was the opportunity to take some of it back: meeting people, having a drink with folk and being with those my own age. Without the disco I would have missed all that.

There are too many disabled folk who are reluctant to move forward, who are caught up in the 'you can't do this, you can't do that' syndrome. They lack confidence or end up believing what people keep telling them. Doing the disco gave me a 'mask', a front to be anyone. DJing is great for self-confidence because you are in control and you decide whether the crowd dances quickly or slowly, alone or as a couple. You are taking people on a journey, making their night something to remember, creating the right atmosphere. You're surrounded by lights, you've got all your tunes at the ready that you know will go down amazingly... you're on top of the world. Thinking about it now, it was a lot of responsibility and not as easy as I thought it would be when I started. You did need to have a brain to do it. It gave me confidence, and a lot more besides. It helped me realise that people are people whatever their disability, they're all the same, whoever they are, or whatever their standing in life.

Of course, I still had all this DJ equipment. I'd had decent use out of it and made some money back, so it owed me nothing. I knew there were people who'd be interested if I stripped it down like some dodgy car and sold the parts off. That didn't seem right though. I mulled it over for a while, then I thought about college and what I'd got out of it, and about the Students Union. Unfortunately, they would never be able to lay their hands on enough money to buy disco equipment and run it, so I did the only decent thing. 'Jonny'll Fix It' stepped in and offered them the equipment so the students could run the discos themselves. For one thing, they wouldn't have to put up with the run-around I went through with the DJs, plus they could put the events on whenever they wanted and continue charging an entrance fee so they could keep up to date with new records. I thought that was a good thing to do.

They came and took it all off my hands and that was it. Job done. I do have a little grievance though. They got all that equipment from me for nothing, but I didn't hear from them for over a year, and that was only to invite me to their reunion, not to say those two little words we're all taught as children. I just wrote back saying no. For one thing, I couldn't afford it at the time, but really I was a little bit narked. I mean, I wasn't looking for a blue plaque on the wall or anything like that. But the Students Union didn't even bother to write to me to say the equipment was great and they appreciated it. Just to let them know how I felt, when I returned the invite I put a sarcastic comment on. Soon after I sent it I got a letter back from the Principal apologising and telling me how grateful they were, and about the extension they were going to build to house the equipment, and how he was going to invite me down to see it when everything was in place. And that was the last I heard. Not a dickie bird more. Except for the reunion invites they sent each and every year. I filed them in the bin.

After doing the discos I got into hospital radio. It was the Health Visitor from Hexham General Hospital who suggested it. I thought it was a great idea, so Mother and I went along to Northumberland Hospital Radio in Wansbeck on the following Sunday to be shown what to do. A presenter was in the middle of her show, and I watched her to pick up a few hints and ideas. She was surrounded by all kinds of equipment — loads of buttons and twiddley bits. After the briefest of inductions, the whole thing seemed pretty straightforward, so when I was asked how soon I would like to start we arranged to begin on the following Monday. And that was it — I was a DJ again!

We got there reasonably early on the Monday, assuming somebody would be there to assist. But the place was deserted. There were a few records lying around, but they weren't exactly to my taste, so we had to sort out some good stuff from their collection. I thought there was no way I would remember everything they had taught us on our crash-course, but I did remember that I must not let the needle on a certain dial go into the red or I would deafen the patients with noise. I cued a few records up that I'd dug out and I was ready for action. Mother and me exchanged glances, then we both tentatively looked at the switch that would knock off Metro Radio and put me on the air.

'Well, I'm here to do it. Let's go for it,' I said.

Mother shrugged, flicked the switch and I was off. I'd brought a record from home to use as my signature tune – Jonathan King's *Johnny Reggae*. I played a bit of that first... *Here comes Johnny Reggae. Here comes Johnny Reggae...* while in between I introduced myself, talked a bit about the show and what kind of day it was. It was all very professional for someone who was still a teenager. From my point of view, the show was much like the movie *Good Morning Vietnam* and I was Robin Williams. I went all out to have a good time and it definitely came across as that to the listeners.

It amazed me how easily I fell into the role. I'd had a CB radio when I was younger, so sitting talking into a microphone to myself was no bother for me at all. I did a few shows and I loved it; talking about this and that and throwing the odd joke in or whatever I'd heard on the radio or TV. Then, with a twinkle in my eye, I decided to bring some characters into it. It was *amazing*. The whole thing just fell into place and really took off. I've no idea where it all came from, it was quite spontaneous.

I was talking this one evening and told the listeners that my cousin Bruce was visiting from Australia and he wanted to say a few words. Then I put on this brusque

Australian accent and yelled: *'G'day! Is anybody there? I hope ya all keepin well!'*

'Bruce, you don't need to shout! They're not deaf. Well, some of them might be, but don't worry about them!'

Of course, 'Bruce' stayed longer than he should, and came back week after week, along with other characters that I introduced. It got to the stage with Bruce when he wanted to take over the whole show and we actually had an imaginary fight on air. You could hear the banging and clattering of a scuffle going on over the top of this record. How I wasn't kicked out of the place, I'll never know.

It was odd working with no sign of a response though. I mean, how did I know if anyone was listening? I just had to continue on regardless and assume I had listeners. Then one day someone rang from one of the wards asking me to turn the sound up. They had no idea how good that made me feel, knowing that someone wanted to hear me. It was grand. Not too long after that phone call, a young DJ on Metro Radio introduced an Australian 'visitor' to his show who just happened to sound like Bruce. *The swine!* I bet they got that from me. It was just too similar not to be. It didn't work for him though. Mine was spontaneous – totally off the cuff – and had comic timing. You could tell his was scripted and, because of that, it didn't work. It was strange to hear it, and I suppose I should have been flattered, but Bruce was *my* cousin, not theirs!

Eventually, my second stint at being a DJ got too much. Travelling to Wansbeck took a lot out of me, and I had to take other people into consideration, too. Not everybody was having as good a time as I was. Father was travelling to and from work, and dropping me off and picking me up as well. It was becoming a hassle and got to the point where I thought I'd give it up for a while. I did hear from our Health Visitor that the head of the hospital had offered to pay my petrol expenses if I ever wanted to go back, and it was nice to feel wanted – they'd obviously had some good feedback about my show. I loved it while it lasted and would have liked a career in something like that. It was great to know that people had enjoyed what I had done and that I'd cheered someone's day up.

Chapter Eight

CONCORDE is the ultimate in passenger flight — total decadence and the fastest ride of your life. The dream of flying on Concorde was still in the back of my mind from my school days. I knew I wasn't gonna get another wish granted like I had at school. The real world isn't like that. So, when the newspaper announced that Concorde would be flying to Newcastle from London, I seized the moment. I had the money, and this was too good an opportunity to let slip by.

My parents left the flight entirely up to me to sort out. Maybe they thought it would put me off the idea, but they should have known that Jonny Kennedy doesn't give up that easily. It was the early 80s, and I was only about sixteen, so even just buying a train ticket to London was quite a responsibility. But I managed it – I travelled by train to London and then flew back to Newcastle on Concorde! London to Newcastle only takes about an hour on a normal plane, so I was careful not to blink in case I missed any of the supersonic flight.

Unfortunately I wasn't in a window seat, which made the actual trip a bit boring. You do get the best of everything on that plane though. There was champagne and caviar, although I must admit I was not impressed with the latter. I do like many of the good things in life, but not all of them – like eating fish eggs, for example. I don't see what people get out of that. I prefer brandy and cigars every time. It was a grand trip though, and as we reached Newcastle the intercom broke into life and the pilot informed us we were gonna do a fly-past. Then he pulled back the throttle (if that's what you do with Concorde's throttle) and we went full-thrust straight up into the sky. We shot up like a rocket. *The power!* Did I say it was boring earlier? Forget that. It pinned me to my seat and was the ultimate in rollercoaster rides. We just went straight up. It was fantastic.

When we touched down and everybody began to get off the plane, I thought I'd hang back a bit. I couldn't miss the opportunity now could I? I told the stewards I was involved with a charity and asked if it would be possible to have a bottle of bubbly to auction. They were only too happy to oblige. I was given two bottles along with other stuff, and had my picture taken with the captain, sitting in his seat in the cockpit. I couldn't get over the amount of switches, dials and gizmos in that place – it was unbelievable. Even the seat was electric.

People from Metro Radio were on the tarmac reporting on the event and, since I was the last passenger off, they asked me what I thought of it. I told them how wonderful it was and that I'd been given all this stuff: champagne, pen, leather luggage label and a mass of other bits and pieces. It must have sounded like I had just come off a quiz show. It was just fantastic. I should have found a way to bring cousin Bruce into the conversation...

Our family has never bought newspapers. They're an unnecessary item. We'd get them from Uncle Bob to use to start the fire up, and it was only then that Mother got a chance to read them. That's what life is like out in the sticks. She was doing the fire one day, when a special offer for a cruise on the QE2 grabbed her attention. It sounded like a good thing so we followed it up and Mother and I booked straight away.

In no time at all we were on our way to New York. We had one night in that amazing city before a bus ride to the port. At first glance the QE2 was a bit disappointing. The Queen Elizabeth 2, the last of the great transatlantic liners... was basically 963 feet of rust. That's my expert opinion. The poor thing looked in desperate need of a paint-job. I felt a bit let down at first because I was expecting this big fine ship to be in pristine condition, not something beyond its sell-by date.

We made our way through port security and then on past balloons and banners to board the ship itself. There were a lot of steps so, once I was onboard and settled, I was quite happy to stay there. On movies you see great liners leaving port with streamers and confetti floating in the wind, but the reality didn't compare. Our departure seemed hastily arranged, with just five or six streamers in total, and a band that must have taken the budget soaring into tens of pounds. So much for romantic movies, eh? Best left in the head, I guess.

We set sail, and were soon out into the ocean. It was grand, looking out and being surrounded by water, in the very middle of nowhere, with nothing to see on the horizon except for the setting evening sun. I suppose it's all part of going on cruises, but for me it was such a bother to dress for dinner. I think that's because you are actually *told* to dress up rather than making the decision yourself. I was a bit tired and just wanted to eat without any hassle. But no, I had to clart on with ties, jackets and things. What a chore.

Now I began to forget about the rusty exterior of the ship. The inside was amazing. It was impossible to fault it.

The food was as good as you'd expect in the finest restaurant in the world, and the service was amazing. But not every detail was perfect. On the first night there wasn't a menu, and you just had to take what was there. There were baked potatoes, and I thought a baked potato with garlic butter would be perfect. Normally, they say whatever the customer wants, the customer gets. 'The customer is always right.' Right? *Wrong.* They couldn't provide garlic butter for me tatty, could they?

One thing that amused me was that you got a 'pudding' after every course. I thought it was great, like being rewarded, as I recalled how Mother used to tell me if I cleared my plate I'd get some pudding. But onboard the QE2, it wasn't really a pudding. It was a *sorbet.* This is what posh people do, apparently. They have a sorbet after each course to clean their palate for the next. Silly me.

I like a good brandy, and am prepared to experiment, so when I saw blackberry brandy on the drinks menu I thought it would have been rude not to sample it. I usually have my brandy with lemonade to spin it out, but this time I thought I'd taste it straight. I had a sniff, swilled it around the glass, and... phew!.. the fumes were worse than the actual drink and nearly took my eyeballs out! I wish I had bought a bottle because I haven't been able to find it anywhere since. It was one heck of a strange brandy and I loved it. It was wicked stuff – and by gum it didn't half warm me up.

Every night after dinner there was a cabaret. And believe me, it could beat anything on land. Big name singers, troupes of dancers, it was beautifully done. I mean, it was really worth going to. I took my camera, but we never seemed to get good seats. All my attempts to photograph it came out with railings across the dancers' heads. But there was one night when we managed to get down to the front. Petula Clark was the star performer and, during one of her numbers, she came over and mingled amongst the crowd. After the show, the floor manager asked if we'd enjoyed it. Wicked old me – I never miss a trick.

'It was very nice of Petula Clark to come across and say hallo,' I said. 'She's somebody I've always wanted to meet.' I was talking crap, but you know – you've got to try.

'Would you like to meet her, properly?' he asked.

'I'd love to,' I said.

Mother was giving me a *'What are you on about?'* look, and I was giving her a *'Why not?'* look in reply. So off we went backstage to meet Petula Clark, and what a little woman she is. I'm no giant, but she was tiny. We had a bit of a chat and got on well. She was very down-to-earth and had plenty of time for us. Mother asked if she could take our photograph too. It was good.

On the nights that we didn't go to the cabaret, we went to the casino to have a little flutter on the roulette wheel. I had no idea what to do, but watched the players that were winning and followed what they were doing. They never put a bet on a number – always on a crossed line – so I did the same. I didn't win too much, but at least I wasn't losing huge sums like some of the others. One night this man asked what my system was and if he could watch me. God, I hardly knew how to play and he made me out to be a professional gambler!

On another night, this woman took the huff with me. She was dripping with diamonds and must have been absolutely minted. She looked like Cruella from *101 Dalmatians*, with the same witchy nose, dark hair and bad attitude to match... and I was sitting in *her* seat. Boy, was she in a bad mood. I could tell she was just waiting, biding her time. I could sense her staring daggers at me all evening. As soon as I was off that stool and had pulled all the daggers out of my back, I turned to see her perched on it, surrounded by chips, and doing some serious gambling. I lost that night, too. Her fault, I'm sure.

Every morning Mother would go swimming by herself, so I'd go onto the deck and sit on one of the loungers and chat to people. That was the life. I mean, I was meeting all sorts of folk from everywhere and we were just getting on. I liked that. Just having everyday conversations and not being gawped at or hassled, enjoying the weather and nice company, or doing my own thing – grand.

I'd felt an urge to bring some Tarot cards with me on the voyage. So here I was this day sitting on deck, playing with them on a table. I was just minding my own business, but it was surprising the interest I got from passing stewards. One or two people came over and had a glance to see what I was doing.

Eventually an American lady came over. 'Do you read the cards?' she asked.

I didn't really, although I had learnt a little bit about them from Father.

'Well, I dabble a bit,' I said. 'Nothing serious, though.'

'Could you tell me about them?' she asked.

There was nothing to lose.

'Yeah, alright. Sit down,' I said. I showed the cards to her and explained a bit about them.

'Could you do me a reading?' she asked.

We got down to it and I did her reading, and she was thrilled. The problem now was, how to put it to her that it was good luck to cross the cards with silver? It was just for fun and all that and I know I had a cheek but I still went for it, explaining how gypsies would cross palms with silver in ancient times, only today it was done in the form of money. She commented that because of the way I was dressed, she knew I wasn't on the scrounge. Then she gave me a dollar. Not bad, eh? Later she wrote a letter to me on Cunard headed paper, saying how wonderful it had been and how she'd enjoyed it, and if I were ever on Staten Island in New York to call her as she'd love another reading. It was good, because it broke the ice and gave me confidence to continue giving readings, which I did and still do.

Mother was busy in the afternoons, too, since there were classes on the QE2 she was interested in. Not for me! I needed to be where people were passing and chatting, just hanging out. I was happiest doing that. I found myself a nice little corner, got my cards out again and did readings for one or two other people. Then I got chatting to this fella who in the past had worked for the New York Police Department drawing photo-fits. He'd got sick of it and got a job on the QE2 as an artist, drawing sketches of passengers. He came across to me and asked for a reading, so we did a swap. I read his cards and he drew my picture!

One day a total stranger came over to me and asked if I'd like to visit the ship's bridge. She'd had the offer from the Captain and thought I might like to go along. Wasn't that nice of her? With an invitation like that you just couldn't stop me. It was an amazing experience. I couldn't believe how small the ship's wheel was. It was more like something on an arcade game than something you'd use to steer such a huge ship. 'Well, where do I put my 10p?' I asked. I'd imagined something big and hefty, a real masculine wheel like you'd see in pirate films. The reality was a tiny thing the size of a dinner plate. I couldn't believe it. It looked stupid on a great big ship like that. Maybe they should have a larger one in a locker for when tourists visit.

There were a few crew members up there, but basically the QE2 drives herself. She's all computerised. You just type in where you want to go and that's it, apparently, although I suppose they keep the complexity of it to themselves. They had a special QE2 stamp, which they use on the crew's passports. Cheekily, I asked if could have my passport stamped with it and off they went and did it. It was great apart from the selling point to actually going to the bridge – the piddley little wheel. What a let down. I'm sure they could afford a bigger one than that, you know.

I bought all my duty free with some winnings off the roulette wheel and money from card readings, and I went well over the top on what you were allowed to take. When I went on holiday – and I hope there are no customs people reading this – I always used to stock up with cigars because I'd never be sure when my next holiday would be. And on board the QE2 they were so cheap I just couldn't let the opportunity go. I had cigars hidden all over the place. I had big boxes of Dutch Masters and King Edwards, and I had my Café Crèmes – they were crammed *everywhere.*

Journey over, we disembarked and, strangely, nobody searched us. I think it was a case of: *Wheelchair! Get it out of the way as quick as possible.* I would have hidden more Duty Free if I'd known we'd be going straight through. They just bundled us into a taxi, and away we went. The whole experience was over just like that. No lingering, no lasting goodbyes. Just off and away.

I would love to do another cruise. My ambition is to sit on the deck of a ship, with a blanket over my legs. There would be a nice warm breeze caressing my cheeks and I'd sit there and watch the sun go down with a brandy, blackberry brandy if I could get it, and cigars by my side. I'd love to stay there all night with just the breeze, the sea air, and the waves against the ship, and I'd be served croissants and hot chocolate while watching the sunrise. Just the job! If I could do that I'd feel like I'd really achieved something.

Chapter Nine

BEING back at Rochester after college wasn't that great. Here I was, stuck out in the middle of nowhere again, although Father did build me a little cottage out of one of the old barns. It was probably his method of getting me out of the way, but I did love my cottage and the bit of independence it gave me. Mother would come over every night to talk over the day and help me into bed. Then in the morning, when she'd fed the chickens, milked the goats, seen to the horses, and sheep if they needed it, she'd come over and help me out of it again.

I couldn't get out of the valley without help, although I could go along to the First and Last pub for a drink, and for some well-needed company. In the country, everybody knows everybody's business, and the First and Last was a hive of activity and gossip. Mind you, you didn't go in there at lambing time unless you wanted to hear all about sheep, and people shoving their hands up sheep's backsides. But everybody met there, and the food was good too. It was a lifeline for me. Everyone knew me and could relax in my company, and I could relax in theirs. It was great!

During the day I would go along to the local café, and that meant a great deal to me. It gave me a purpose and a reason to get out of bed in the morning. It was just great to go down there, to see everybody and catch up with what was going on. The owners of the caff, Ruth and Keith never seemed to mind me sitting in the corner chatting to folk as they passed through. I liked Ruth and Keith a lot and we all got on very well, but they were the oddest couple you'd ever wish to meet. They were the epitome of chalk and cheese. Ruth was very laid back and easy going; as long as she had a coffee and a fag in her hand, the world could just get on with itself. Keith was definitely the opposite; people just never knew which way to take him, and he could sometimes be like a stick of dynamite ready to go off. I'm not sure that was his fault, because he suffered from diabetes and I think that may have affected his moods. But I take as I find, so I just took his moods a bit like taking the weather.

The thing that people never got to see about Keith was that he had a very big heart and was a very kind man. I remember going down there one day when he'd read this article in the paper about the use of cannabis to control pain, and we got into discussing whether it would help me. I told him I'd try anything if I thought I could get some relief but I didn't know where I'd be able to get a hold of anything like cannabis, and neither did he. He'd heard you could get it abroad, so suggested we have a weekend away in Amsterdam. I was surprised and touched when he said that, knowing how busy he was running the café. Maybe he needed a holiday. Of course it didn't take me long to agree, and, like a man with a mission, he went away to arrange it.

The big weekend soon came, and we set off to catch the ferry. His car wasn't the best and, as usual with such adventures, there were problems. Halfway to Hull, the engine overheated with smoke bellowing out. We pulled into the nearest garage and found that the hose to the radiator had split. I think Keith was glad of the break from driving, for he didn't blow his top once and took it all in his stride. There was no waiting room or anywhere you could go for a coffee at the garage, so I stayed in the car while all this was going on.

When the young mechanic finished replacing the hose he jumped into the driving seat to test it and off we went. It didn't seem too bad at first, until, that is, we took off shooting down the road at speeds I never thought that car was capable of doing. In the mechanic's hands, it was a racing car. I even had to lean to one side to stop us going over on two wheels when we negotiated a roundabout. Phew! We were back in the garage in no time. The mechanic switched the ignition off and said with a smile, 'Well, no problems there then!' I just sat there numb – stunned into silence. Keith got back in, and off we went.

Once in Hull and onboard the ferry, we had a bit of time while waiting to sail. And it wasn't until then that Keith realised his big mistake. He hadn't booked a cabin for us and there was nowhere available to lie down. Boy, was this gonna be a long night. Like a lost soul, I searched the ship trying to get somewhere comfortable for my aching body to rest, relieved that at least the seas we were sailing through were calm. I was so pleased when light broke and the PA system crackled into life, introducing us to Holland. Within the hour we had disembarked and were off driving into the wilds of that flat land.

I recall taking in the scenery and thinking, 'So far so good!' I must have soon dozed off, because the next thing I knew I was being abruptly woken, with a map thrust in front of me. I looked at Keith, who'd just discovered road rage, and I knew things weren't boding well. He was getting into the foreign way of driving, jumping up and down on the horn and swearing at the cars in front. I looked at the map and tried to get our bearings. How was I going to break it to my unstable companion that we were going the wrong way? I didn't feel this was going to be a good moment in our adventure, but we managed to get through it without mayhem. I did my best to work out the route and get us on the right track, and before long we were in the city of Amsterdam. We found our hotel and, once in our room, we crashed out, totally exhausted.

The next day, we rose bright and early and hit the town. The sun was shining and the day was cool. It was so nice just to be looking around and taking it all in. I remembered watching a program on TV about the use of cannabis in Holland. There was a café featured in it that was quite prominent, and it didn't take us long to find it. We went in like a couple of cool dudes, took a seat, and started off by having a coffee.

It was fine to ease into things but, not wanting to waste any more time, I said to Keith, 'This isn't really what we came for. Where do you think we can get the *stuff* from?'

'I know as much as you,' he replied. 'But I'll go and see if I can find out more information.'

So off he went. He returned a few minutes later with what looked like a large suppository. He revealed his vast knowledge of drug-taking: if we felt sick after taking the first few drags we needed to have something to eat. Food is usually the last thing on my mind when I feel sick, but Keith seemed to know the score. He handed me the joint and lit it... it was now or never... the moment of truth. I took the joint and tentatively took a couple of drags.

'That's not gonna get you very far,' he said. 'You need to inhale it, deeply.'

It seemed that Keith was now an expert. I took a long drag... it was like breathing in sixteen garden fires all at once. The taste was terrible and it burnt my throat and chest like nothing I had ever known before, and my eyes watered from being surrounded by the smoke. I thought smoking this stuff was supposed to get rid of the pain, not increase it! I couldn't see what there was to gain from it at all; it certainly didn't make me want to get into using it regularly.

I composed myself and sat for a minute until the cannabis took effect. My body soon relaxed, and all I wanted to do was sit. And sit. I didn't even have the energy to lift my arms. I smacked my lips and felt my eyelids getting heavier, my head panning around the room, with my vision following behind, my eyes unable to focus on anything. It was a strange sensation, a bit like alcohol without the dizziness.

Now, full of bravado, Keith decided he would have a go himself. He was an ardent smoker, a 40-a-day man for many years, so reckoned he'd show me how it was done. He took the joint and inhaled deeply. From my perspective, it was like the ignition of Mount Vesuvius. He went many different colours; his eyes enlarged and began to water. He started spluttering, and smoke seemed to appear from every orifice as he began to cough – and *boy* was he coughing.

He'd suffered from a bad heart for years, and this was certainly putting it to the test. I was so sure he wasn't going to make it, and my thoughts quickly turned to how much money I had to get home! I pushed my coffee towards him, but the more I pushed the longer it took, everything was moving in slow motion. In between the gasps for air, Keith managed to drink some coffee. I doubt caffeine was the best thing for him, although some degree of normality seemed to re-appear. Thank goodness. I really thought he was a goner that time. I think he did too.

We enjoyed our time in Holland though, and did the 'sights', as all men would be expected to do. Keith continued turning funny colours, but he hung in there and we made it. Taking me to Amsterdam was one of the best things he could have ever done for me. I had the chance to try something else that might have helped my condition, and I have Keith to thank for it. We both knew it was an excuse for a weekend away and it was great just to be a bit daft for a while. I did try smoking cannabis a couple of times at a later date, but I just couldn't get away with inhaling the smoke.

Life's a strange old thing. I can't count the number of times it's made me cry into my pillow. I could sit forever, searching for answers, asking, wondering. What am I looking for? Proof, I suppose. Proof that there is a God, that there is something else after this. But there are no answers, no replies, nothing. I do believe in a God, but I've never really settled on any particular religion. I've tried different ones, and I've taken little bits from each of them, a bit like a pick 'n' mix I suppose. I know in my heart what I believe in, and I'm content with that now. But, by gum, it's been quite a journey to get to this point.

My parents were Spiritualists and we'd go to their church. My family have always been ones who have searched and looked. Orthodoxy really hasn't given them the answers they are looking for. Mother was brought up a Christian Scientist but, basically, it wasn't enough for her. Her search continued, and she found the Spiritualist Church. I was first taken along when I was about four years old, and I'm still a member of the church today, but that hasn't stopped me looking elsewhere.

Spiritualists believe that there is something after this life – a higher plane of existence. That's where your spirit goes after you die. So at the Spiritualist Church, after the prayers and the sermon and the hymns, you get a medium contacting these spirits of the dead and receiving messages and guidance. It can be a right barrel of laughs, I can tell you. If I sound cynical, it's because I've become cynical. I'm looking for answers, but no one can give me them.

For years Mother and Father held a spiritualist healing circle at the farm. None of it really floated my boat. Father did Tarot cards, and he taught me how to read them, but, to be honest, you can adapt your mind to see, approve and accept anything. Snippets did get through the cracks in my armour, but still my boat wouldn't float. We'd go to spiritualist fairs all over the place and I'd have the cards read, and everything else that was on offer. Although I was still searching for answers, it was more a case of something to do than anything else.

I went to Lourdes when I was a lad, of course, but that meant nothing more than a free holiday to me. I was trying something I didn't really understand. Maybe if I went back there today it would be different, but honestly, I never saw any miracles, never saw anyone get any answers then, so why would they today? So my search for answers continued through my teenage years. Why did God do this to me? Why was I picked out to suffer?

Then my friend Roger started coming up to Rochester and staying over. That sort of thing had never happened before and you have no idea how good that made me feel — someone actually staying here for me. It was phenomenal, because up until then there were times when I'd see no one for months on end. I suspect Father had moved us up here so we wouldn't be near anyone, so no one could see me and so no one would associate my condition with him. That was the extent of his embarrassment. Anyway, Rog appeared and we'd spend the day crying and laughing before going over to the farmhouse for lunch or dinner, then maybe pop down to the pub for a drink. They were great times because together we'd analyse spirituality to try to get to the truth.

It wasn't all about theology though. Far from it. I remember one night at the pub when I'd made it there in my buggy. It was a summer night and my buggy is really slow, so Father took Rog there in the car. Father wouldn't stay for a drink with us, so Rog was inside waiting for me when I arrived in my usual style – fashionably late. The night was great, and the pub was full of friends from my short experience at school, now all grown up. We talked to everyone and had a right old laugh before rolling out a little worse for wear at closing time.

So there I was, in my buggy, covered up and absolutely fine. Snug as a bug, driving home, albeit slightly less-controlled than usual. However, it was another story for poor old Rog, who had to run the three miles back to Rochester alongside me with just the light of my buggy to show us the way. The last thing he wanted to do after a drinking session was to go for a jog. The only thing that could have made it any worse for him would have been if it had rained. Which it did. Rog was puffing away by my side, getting soaked through and trying not to get knocked over, when all of a sudden he disappeared. It was bizarre.

Of course, he hadn't really disappeared. Rog had run up the road towards the farm, but I, being so drunk and busy laughing at him, had missed the turn-off and mistakenly headed down into the village. I was oblivious to all this, while Rog was also in the dark – lost and fumbling his way back as there are no street lights out in the country. We both made it back to the farm in one piece eventually, although I can't quite remember how!

One of the many things Father was into was numerology. It's often placed alongside stuff like astrology, is sometimes associated with the occult, and is basically about having a belief in numerical patterns and looking at the relationship between numbers and people. One day after lunch, he asked Rog if he could do his numbers. Rog agreed and began to provide Father with all the details of his life: address, area code, National Insurance number, the lot – everything he and Father could think of that had a number associated with it. Numerology means reducing all these numbers to a single digit, and no matter what Rog gave him, Father always came up with the same answer – number one. This seemed so strange that Father couldn't believe it! Thinking he'd got it wrong, he went through it all again and again before asking Rog for more information to calculate. Again, they all reduced to number one. This was supposed to mean Rog was an 'individual' or an 'aggressor' or a 'Yang'. Rog just smiled at father: 'Yes, Frank. Whatever! *Whatever!*' he said, as we headed out of the kitchen. Father never asked him for numbers again... so I never got the chance to make a note of all his bank details and PINs!

As I say, I am a bit of a cynic, but I'll try anything once, just in case. I think you've got to knock on every door to find what you're looking for and you never know unless you try, right? If you stop searching you'll never find it. I got well into crystals and all the hype surrounding their powers – I was curious to see what they were about and if they really worked. The belief in crystal power has been around since the time of the ancient Egyptians, and it is said that they have energy and vibrate at different frequencies. Crystals can supposedly help retune you and rebalance your body's energies – something like that, anyway. Who am I to argue? If the Egyptians could build pyramids and stuff that have stood for a couple of thousand years and no one knows how they did it, they must have been pretty clued up. Before long, I had quite a collection of crystals, including a huge amethyst geode bigger than myself. I also had a brass frog with a coin in its mouth that someone said would bring me money if people rubbed it. I don't miss a trick. And *everyone* has to rub the frog. I'm not kidding – if you don't rub the frog, you're not getting in.

I've kept up with Spiritualism because the family are still into it. It's a comfort to them. But I'm not interested in just accepting huge spiritual concepts... 'this is the right path to take'... whatever. All I've ever wanted was a bit of peace; respite from the constant pain. It was my deep talks with Rog in my little bungalow in Rochester that seemed to put things into perspective and order. Apart from the subject of spirituality interesting us both, our search began because talking about myself became so heavy at times. Rog would change the subject to take my mind off all the other stuff – mainly Father. So back in his flat in Newcastle Rog would read and research, and in my cottage in Rochester we'd talk and pull different ideas and theories to bits.

Mother would also read to me because I'm not very good at reading books. I can't hold them easily and certainly can't turn a page – it's far too much trouble, and in the end not worth the effort. I'd find tapes to listen to and watch the odd video. So it was Rog who did all the homework; *The Talmud, Torah, Al-Cur'an, Bible, Bhagavad Gita, Maha Barata*, secret sects, magic rituals, whirling dervishes, Sai Baba, Sanskrit Sutras, Kuhani the ancient path of the Hawaiian and so many more – they all have their place and all work perfectly well for those drawn to them. That's why they're there. But me, I wanted more. How about the truth? How about God? How about why I'm here, and who the hell am I anyway?

Ultimately, it was science that gave us some of the answers we were seeking. I think it's well-documented that the universe is dual – two of everything within it. It's endless when you begin to look; black and white, up and down, night and day, tall and small, thin and fat, a hill and a dip.

So this universe of ours always has kept, and always will keep, us in order by the concept and truth of balance. That's karma, yin and yang, Isaac Newton's law of balance... you create shit and, somewhere down the line, you get it back.

So you've got to watch yourself, think about how you live your life, 'cos if you don't do it right it could come back and bite you on the bum. I think you've got to be pretty shallow-minded if you think that we're just born and we die, we just live this life and then that's it. I believe inside that after I die I'll become a spirit again, and my soul will be free. This body I'm in, it's just a shell − a dodgy shell. There's got to be more to life than this mortal coil. There's *got* to be more, otherwise I'll have gone through 36 years of pain and suffering for nowt. And that would be pointless.

So I believe in a God, and I believe there's something else in store for us after we die. I believe we're all sent down here to learn lessons, and I was sent down to this big class-room on Earth to learn what it's like to be in constant pain and discomfort for an entire lifetime. I think I've learnt my lesson, I think I've come to terms with the discomfort and the frustration, and I've learnt to deal with how people react to me, like people in the street and my Father. It was a long journey, but I'm content now with what I believe, and that's how I've found my peace.

Chapter Ten

ONE thing I always looked forward to through school and growing up was learning to drive. I knew when I did that I would truly have my independence. Since my brother was a couple of years older than me, I learnt the Highway Code and stuff through him. I was raring to get behind the wheel.

But there was a problem. When I was younger, I was playing with some dead leaves at school when I fell over and got a leaf stalk caught in my eye. My eyes are like the rest of my body and are prone to get blisters too, so it was not a nice experience. It left a smallish scar and at the time I never thought anything more about it because that sort of thing happens to me all the time, every day.

Then we moved out to Rochester where we had a

Rayburn fire in the kitchen. It was probably dust from the fire but, whatever it was, I got a sharp pain in my eye that lasted for a couple of days, and then a blister appeared. Obviously, doctors couldn't do anything about it since you can't burst a blister on your eye, or bandage it for that matter. And luckily Mother and Father didn't come after me trying to nip that one! I had to wear an eye patch for a couple of weeks and it aggravated the scar and made it worse. This happened around the time that I was learning to drive, so I thought I'd better get my eyes tested. I passed the test, but I couldn't read a number plate at the specified distance except under good light. I was informed that the driving instructor wouldn't even get in the car with me unless I could do that. My dream of learning to drive was ruined.

I was devastated. I really was. I mean, that was just everything to me. Living so far away in the country may seem ideal, but to me it was like being in prison. It was so boring, with no one around except Mother and Father, and even they weren't always there. That's why it was so refreshing to have friends like Roger come visit. Being able to drive would have meant I could escape from my boredom and visit friends if and when I wanted. I used to dream of having that kind of liberty to go places I wanted to, to do things when I wanted to do them, but even that was taken away, and it really got to me. But I had to accept it.

Father would always say that if there was anything I wanted to do or anywhere I wanted to go, he'd take me. The reality would be that I'd tell him I wanted to go to the pictures or something and he'd say, 'Really? Today? The car's been out twice this week already. I'm off to the coast on Thursday. Can you not do it then?' All this would go on and on and I'd end up not bothering.

Eventually I did get an invalid carriage, which was sort of half-car, half-scooter, and I drove here and there and everywhere around the area. The freedom was just great. I began driving back and forward to Alnwick – a round trip of 70 miles at a top speed of only 10 miles per hour! But I was never in any great hurry, it was all about getting there. I even drove down the A1 once. Don't know if I should have or not, but I did it and no one stopped me.

I visited friends in Alnwick, and they were always on at me about getting a proper car and learning to drive, and I had to explain to them about the scar on my eye. But that had been a few years ago, and they pointed out that it might have healed and my vision might have improved. Eventually, after much nagging, I began to wonder if they could be right. There was only one way to find out. I went to another optician and passed with flying colours! I was thrilled, and thought, 'This is it!' I hadn't been allowed to drive in my teens, which was probably a good thing, but now, 'Yippee!'

Of course, I couldn't just go out and buy any old car. Oh,

if only life were that simple, eh? I had to go to a special assessment centre for disabled drivers, which was £40 for the afternoon. In their literature, they boasted specially adapted cars and a test track. Great! Get me behind that wheel. I could hardly wait.

When I arrived there was an instructor monitoring me. They had a car indoors to test my stopping reactions, and everything was going along grand until I got outside and looked for the test track. I was confused. There *was* no track. There was just a field next to a hospital. Driving on grass is not easy no matter what vehicle you're in. It's just a hard thing to do, especially when driving slowly in a specially adapted car. I could drive it up and down the field, but it was an effort, and the instructor was busily writing stuff down on his pad. That makes you paranoid, anyway.

When the instructor asked me why I hadn't learnt to drive earlier, I explained the situation, and told him that I had been back to an optician and proved my eyes were able to cope.

'Alright,' he said. 'Can you read that number plate over there?'

I couldn't. It seemed a lot further than the specified distance, too.

'Well, that's it,' he said. 'There's no point in going on any further.'

And that was the end of that. I just couldn't believe it. I

thought fate had literally stomped on me. I mean, they did it the first time when I was 16 and I was devastated then, but to let me get a bit older and go all that distance just to be kicked in the teeth again seemed totally unfair. At home I had brochures and leaflets about cars and I'd dream of going here and there and even sleeping in it. Trying again had all been for nothing. Except perhaps, to let me down.

It was a bad day for Jonny Kennedy. What had I done? Why should this happen? I'd been through it once already. Why should I have to go through it again? What was that teaching me?

As I sat there in the car, with the instructor standing waiting for my reaction, I saw two porters come from the hospital, pushing a trolley with a white sheet covering it. It was a windy day, and the sheet blew right up in the air, revealing a person lying there. A dead person. That just topped the day off perfectly.

When you are involved with a charity, you get newsletters from them keeping you up to date with what's going on. I received one that advertised what they called 'DebRA Dares'. It just so happened that one of the dares was a sponsored parachute jump. I read and re-read it, and a twinkle appeared in my eye... a plan was being hatched in my mind. No one had ever thought I could do such a thing, because it would go totally against everything that my condition stands for: soft skin, delicateness, blistering. But it was something I had always wanted to do. There are plenty of things I can't do, so when there's something I *want* to do, no one can stop me. I read the newsletter article out loud to Mother and Father. To their minds it just wasn't possible, and they responded by saying that the jump would be for those involved with the charity rather than those with the condition. Never mind, I wasn't disheartened. It was the reaction I was expecting and they didn't put me off. I chucked the newsletter to one side for the time being, and then when I was alone I rang the charity to find out more about it.

I contacted the Appeals Director who rang the parachute centre down in Shropshire, and they put me straight. They said I could not do the jump. Apparently, having EB meant that the cold would affect my hands and I might not be able to pull the ripcord. My heart sank, but only for a moment, because then they told me there was a possibility of doing a tandem jump. They were keen that I should do it too, and sent me all the relevant information. The only hurdle at this stage was getting a doctor's certificate saying I was fit to do it.

My own doctor thought about it for a while. The problem is my condition is so rare that nobody knows what I am actually capable of doing and not doing because there's no real history of it, no case studies, no experience. No one like me had done this before. So I got a letter from the doctor's surgery, which stated that they were concerned about the jump, but that at the end of the day it was my decision. So they weren't saying yes, but they weren't saying no, either. I rang them to clarify and they did say I could do it, as long as I realised it could mean a stay in hospital afterwards. Surely, for the amount of money it would raise for DebRA, it would be worth it? I sent a letter off to the parachute centre, and they were quite happy about the whole thing. I was gonna jump out of a plane!

From there, it was a case of getting everything together, and generating sponsorship and publicity. I got in touch with The Journal newspaper in Newcastle, and the Hexham Courant, and also the local TV stations. They lapped it up, and followed the story to the end. I got really good coverage.

The day of the jump arrived, and I was raring to go. I wore a jumpsuit, and over the top of that I wore what can only be described as a sheepskin leotard (yes, *really*) that went around the crotch area, up my back, and over my shoulders. Then I wore another jumpsuit on top of all that. Plus, I had to wear a helmet and goggles. As for shoes, I wear a size six on my left foot and a size five on my right, and they have to be soft, so I couldn't put any boots on for the jump. I wore a pair of Father's climbing socks over my normal shoes to keep them from being blown into oblivion!

I looked like the Michelin Man as I wobbled out to the

plane where everyone was waiting to greet me. Others had been doing static line jumps from two thousand feet, which they had completed by the time I'd arrived. I was doing a tandem jump with an experienced instructor, so we were gonna jump from ten thousand feet. *Ten thousand* – can you imagine such a height? It would take us half an hour to get up to it. Mother filmed it all with a video camera, but Father couldn't handle any of it and stayed at home.

The instructor was sitting on the ledge of the plane's doorframe when I arrived. I would be attached to his chest, so would essentially be in the front as we fell, and my cynical side told me I'd hit the ground first should anything go wrong. The instructor began telling me how to get into position and get out of the plane, and that his biggest concern was where I should put my feet.

'Make sure your feet go to the right of the step,' he said, 'or the wind will just blow you away. Also, cross your arms so there is nothing you can knock.' No pressure then. As we took off I kept thinking of his words over and over... *Cross your arms, feet to the right of the step. Cross your arms, feet to the right of the step.*

The plane's interior was cold and bare and we sat on the floor. There were two others jumping with us and, when we reached ten thousand feet, out they went, gone in a split-second. Then the pilot began to circle the plane so we could take our time. There was just us and the clouds... *Cross your arms, feet to the right of the step.*

Harnessed together, we shuffled towards the edge of the door. The wind rushed past our heads to such a degree I couldn't hear a word that the instructor said. I put my right foot out first. Now, if you have ever put your hand out of a fast car, you have an idea of what happened next. My foot went *whoosh* to the right, and the force was such that if I hadn't had Father's socks on, that shoe would be in Wales now. I stuck the other foot out, which also got *whooshed* along to the right. Then the instructor climbed out onto the step.

Here we were in a little biplane, sitting on the step of the door under the wing, poised to jump. I looked straight down to see what the distance was and there was no fear in me at all. I was looking forward to it. I'm sure people will think I'm a liar, but you had to be there. With the cold and the wind engulfing me, the instructor tapped me on the shoulder, and together we just... *went.*

The initial rush was just like going down the first hill of a rollercoaster; you lose your stomach before you settle into the ride and equalise. The instructor did tell me not to worry about breathing, to just breathe normally – which I thought was okay since I do that every day. But I don't jump out of a plane every day! We fell five thousand feet in thirty seconds, and I'm supposed to breathe normally?! I had my head turned to one side, because I felt sure I'd be able to grab a bit of air that way. It was difficult. The pressure on my chest was tremendous, too. I was taking the speed of the wind for both of us and thought my chest was going to cave in. The instructor told me to put my arms out, but I did a stupid thing – although it seemed natural at the time. When you feel pain, it's automatic to put your hands where it hurts to try and relieve it. So I put my hands on the straps across my chest, trying to loosen them, thinking they were the problem. With hindsight, this was probably the silliest thing I could have done, because I might have ended up doing a bit of free falling...

It seemed like we were up there for ages. It was only about thirty seconds, but when you have a lack of oxygen it seems like a very long time. Then the instructor said he'd wrap his arms around me and pull the chute, so we'd take the strain together. He tapped my shoulder to let me know what was gonna happen, and – *whoosh* – the chute opened and it felt like we were being dragged back upwards. The chute opening was the part I was dreading, but it wasn't bad at all. The amount of padding around me caused no friction whatsoever. The only bother I had was from the helmet strap, because we hadn't considered that as a threat. There was a bit left flapping, and at that speed it was like a whip, so it did cause friction.

Once the chute was open we just hung in the air. All I could hear was the wind whistling past my ears. It was surreal. It was rush hour below, but we were too high to hear traffic or even birds. The sky was clear and the sun was shining. It was beautiful. We just drifted, calmly. The instructor was in full control manoeuvring us to the left and then to the right, and then we swung round and round as we came down to land. It was like a fairground ride! He kept the chute to the right and we just spun. It was absolutely amazing. Marvellous stuff.

We were still travelling at some speed towards the ground, but he pulled his cords and we immediately slowed down. We had a special spot to aim for, and he guided us in to land. Everybody was there on the ground ready and waiting for us. Having me strapped to his chest made the instructor top heavy, and he would have fallen forwards and squashed me if no one had been there to steady us. But someone grabbed his back, and another person grabbed me, then another ran to the chute just in case the wind took it and dragged us along the ground. It was absolutely mega! They even brought a van to pick us up. Everybody was really happy for me, and it was a great success. It was a brilliant experience and, most importantly, I made it down without injuring myself. The landing was so smooth I would have caused more trauma to my feet jumping off the bottom stair back home!

Chapter Eleven

WE weren't a very big family. Apart from Mother, Father, my brother Simon and myself, there was Granny, her sister Auntie Georgina, Uncle Bob and Uncle Denys. There always seems to be a time in families when you start losing them. And boy, when one goes they all seem to go – like a pack of cards. The only time I'd ever been sad about death was when I lost my cat Terbie, because she was the best pet I ever had. Dealing with people dying is another story altogether.

In 1992, Granny became too ill to live by herself, and moved in with us. That was a bad year for me, to the point where even the doctors thought that was it. Granny came down with shingles, and I never thought any more about it until I started to become really tired and began getting pains in my legs, my glands and up my left side. The doctor said I couldn't have caught shingles, although people with experience of the illness said I probably could. But doctors know everything don't they? *Not!*

One day in particular I felt really poorly, and the pain shooting down my leg was unbearable. And believe me, after all these years, I can usually handle pain. It was like an electric shock. I got up and stripped off (it was bandage day) to find I was covered in spots – spots from the shingles I couldn't catch. Then things went from bad to worse. The doctor put me on painkillers.

Painkillers have never done much to eradicate pain for me, and these ones were no different. Then I got even worse. I was sick and I was off my food, and had no energy whatso-ever. At this point people were getting very worried because it looked like I was starting to waste away. Eventually the doctor put me on morphine, but even that didn't really stop the pain. I was so ill I couldn't walk anywhere and could barely move my limbs. I couldn't even pick up a cup to take a drink.

Mother would come over to my little cottage in the morning with a cup of coffee, but she was helping with the lambing at another farm so didn't have time to get me out of bed, and I'd just have to lie there until she came back. Even if I needed the toilet I just had to wait, because I didn't have the physical strength to do anything by myself. Thank goodness she was only away in the mornings. As if it couldn't get worse than all that, I was hallucinating, too.

Everyone thought I was finished that year. I meet some people now and they still say they thought I'd given up. But somehow I got through it. There were times when I was afraid, too. I said earlier that I wasn't frightened of death, but I've always said it depends on the way you go. It was too soon for me. I was only 25 and I knew life had more in store for me, and yet I was slipping away and didn't know what to do. I panicked and maybe that was possibly what pulled me through it all, I don't know. I wasn't ready to give up just yet. In time I recovered, dusted myself down and got on with it like I've always done. But others in the family continued to slip away.

Auntie Georgina was a very independent woman who'd lived on her own in Whitley Bay for many years. But, when she got older and needed looking after, she came to live with us in the country, too. That was a shock and a half for her. No more playing whist or bridge, or meeting up with friends and having a good old gossip. Poor soul – another brought out to the country prison.

We tried to make things the best we could for her under the circumstances, but you could tell she wasn't happy. She began to sleep a lot, then kept having mini strokes, which meant she had to have spells in hospital. Auntie didn't like being in hospital at all. She'd have wanted to just pass away in her own home, without any fuss being made of her. Eventually she became too much for Mother to look after, especially as I needed caring for as well. It was decided by social workers that she would be better off in residential care back down in Whitley Bay, nearer to the people she knew. I guess all the moving around took its toll. Auntie just seemed to get worse and worse.

During this time my Uncle Bob, who was in his nineties, seemed to be fading away, too. But he was determined to stay in his own home in Whitley Bay to the bitter end, and made my dad promise that under no circumstances would he let anyone take him away and put him in hospital or residential care. To his credit, Father kept his promise and actually moved down to Whitley Bay to help Bob out. This was the first time I ever saw Father look after someone. He had the district nurse come in to see to Uncle Bob's personal needs and made sure Bob was always fed and watered. And I'll give him his due – he made sure Bob got his wish to die at home.

I remember the morning that Bob died, in June 1996, when Father rang to tell us the sad news. Mother and I drove down there to find Father sitting in his car outside Bob's house. We went in together, and there was Bob lying on his side, all skin and bone and as stiff as a board. For a long time he'd been unable to climb the stairs, so Father had set up a bed downstairs for him. The trouble was that Bob was in the living room, next to the telephone, and calls needed to be made. Mother didn't feel comfortable having

Bob in the same room, so it was decided to move him. Father couldn't move Bob on his own, and there was no way Mother was going to help him. Of course, it was down to me to help.

Father put his hands under Bob's arms, and as he sat him up the air leaving Bob's lungs made a kind of *Errrr* sound. I looked at Father and he looked at me.

'He is dead, isn't he?' I asked.

After this was confirmed, I lifted Bob's feet and off we went, shuffling across the room with Father walking backwards, leading the way. Bob's house was narrow and, when we got to the door, Father banged Bob's head off the door jamb.

'Slow down, Cato,' I said. 'Bob has enough problems without having a bump on his head.'

And we both nearly fell about laughing. Finally, we got him onto his new bed but when we laid him on his back, his legs stuck up into the air. I pushed down on them and he sat up again. It was like a comedy sketch. We called to Mother and she brought lots of pillows to make Bob at least *look* comfortable.

When it had become inevitable that Uncle Bob wouldn't last much longer, I had been given the job of ringing around to find the best deal for the funeral. I found a new thing called a woodland funeral where you are laid to rest in a cardboard coffin. There's no headstone, just a plaque on the grass with your name on it, and an oak tree planted in your memory. Eventually, the area is destined to become woodland where people can walk and have fun. I decided that felt right for Bob.

The funeral was in Hexham, so we had to take Bob back up to the farm in the back of Father's Ford Sierra. It was the furthest Bob had been for years – it's just a pity he couldn't appreciate the scenery. Once there, Father didn't feel comfortable having Bob in the house so he was put in the barn, where the feed was kept for the animals. Anyway, it was cool in there.

That night, when I was tucked up in bed, I heard the sound of the door opening downstairs in my cottage and someone coming up the stairs towards the bedroom. No lights went on, and I shouted 'Who's there?' a couple of times without reply. When the door opened I just about hit the ceiling with shock... No, it wasn't Bob coming back to haunt me, it was Father (just as bad!). He stood silently in the dark, leaning against the doorframe. It was quite unnerving.

I couldn't understand why Father was there or what he wanted, until eventually he started to speak, 'I just want to thank you for today,' he said in a very strange, awkward way. 'You made things a lot easier. You lightened the situation, and I don't know if I could have coped had you not been there.'

Poor Dad, he was really struggling to get the words out. I had never been in a situation like that with him before. For the first time in my life we were having a father/son relationship. He was my dad and it was amazing. He hadn't taken things for granted after all. However, after he'd got the words out he just left without waiting for my reply. I think it was one of those moments when saying nothing meant more, and I probably would have made a bollocks of things anyway. It wasn't until many months later – and I mean many months – that I told Mother that Father had been over to thank me. It had been a moment I'd never forget.

The next day was the day of the funeral and Father had the job of taking Bob in the Sierra while we all followed in a car behind him. I felt it was the most personal funeral that you could ever have. I think Bob would have been proud. It was the first time the undertaker in the Hexham cemetery had seen a family do the whole funeral themselves. Maybe it looked a bit haphazard and rough around the edges but, let's face it, life isn't perfect, so why should death be?

When Father said he was going to look after Bob it had surprised Mother and me, because throughout my life he had never helped her to look after me. But he had looked after Bob, and he had done a really good job. And I know he really appreciated my help after Bob died. I only wish Dad had been able to see me as the person I am more than just that one time, for this new-found closeness just came a bit too late for us.

It wasn't that we ever discussed it, but he just couldn't cope with my condition. We shared a relationship that was mixed with love and hate. Father hated that he didn't know how to deal with my condition and hated what it had done to me and the family. I think he thought that me being the way I am challenged his masculinity somehow and found the whole situation of me and my condition an embarrassment. In the grand scheme of things, he didn't get it – he didn't get what life was all about. If we're sent down to learn lessons, he didn't learn his.

Just a week after Uncle Bob died, Auntie Georgina passed away. And, within months of Bob and Georgina dying, it was Father's turn to take that journey.

Father was diagnosed as having angina and walked out of the consultation room into the waiting area and said to us, 'I'm finished.' From that day on he just went downhill, until he died of a heart attack in January 1997 at the age of 62. Just as he had said, he thought he was finished, he thought it was a death sentence. He gave up.

Before the year was out, Granny had died, too. Like I said, when one goes, they all go.

There were times when I was younger that I'd think about death, and I must admit I still do today. What will it be like? Will it be painful? Will it take a long time? Or will it be just *nothing*, just sleep. I'd wondered if I was the only one who considered death, or did everybody think about it? I certainly visited some dark places.

I hated not being able to live life the way my brother had. When we were boys, I'd watch him out of the window. He'd be out playing with his friends and I just yearned to be out there with them. But every time I tried to play I just ended up knacking myself. The furthest I got in those days was either the back garden or the side yard. My parents told me it was for my own good, although I didn't appreciate that back then. I still don't. Time and time again I'd ask why I couldn't go out, and the standard reply was that I might get hurt.

My parents did their best when I was younger but it was quite a lonely existence. I had my own toys and had to make my own entertainment. As I got older it did change a bit. I made my own friends, but there was many a day I'd go into deep depression because of the constant pain and struggles. You can have a million friends and still be depressed.

I went to school with lots of disabled kids, and saw other people getting on with their problems and their lives. I think that's how I got to the stage of just coping. If others could cope, then so could I. That's life. You just have to get on with it, don't you? But I did think a lot about what it would be like just to be dead.

When we lived in Whitley Bay I'd come in tired from school and go straight to my room and lie down on my bed. I'd try to shut everything out. I'd imagine death, because all I wanted at the time was to be free from the suffering. I just wanted to be away from it all without consequence. Every day seemed to throw up another problem or pain. I would see somebody else doing something I couldn't do and it would just set me off wondering. Is this it? Is this what it's gonna be like all my life? Being shown I can't do this or I can't do that? Why aren't there miracles? You read in the Bible that there are miracles, that God can do miracles, that people can be healed. So what's wrong with me? Why should I be left out? Why should I have to suffer every day, every night?

As I got older, things started falling into place. I eventually came to the conclusion that taking my life was just not the right way to go. Life is for living and you are here on Earth to learn a lesson. Life works out better for some than for others, but you have to experience it whatever, you have to learn. If I chickened out and left the classroom before my time, I'd be sent right back and I'd have it all to do again... and that was the last thing I wanted.

So now, at 36 years of age, I'm still here. The pain goes on. The bandaging goes on. EB takes most sufferers to about middle age, so I've not got long left. There are times, you know – and I don't tell Mother because it would just upset her – that I crave for when I pass away, I die. I know inside that there is some sort of life after death, and then later reincarnation, but I'm not even worried about that. I just want to get away from the hurt – to be at peace. I just don't want to go on with this forever and ever. No person could endure it. I've taken it all these years and I suppose I'll have to put up with it for a bit longer yet. So, everything being as it is, I will carry on. But, oh, for that day when there is just *nothing*.

Then there are times when I think about my own funeral. Like most people, I hate funerals. I've been to a few and I don't like them. It doesn't seem right. You go out in such a stupid way in a wooden box and you're either stuck in a six-foot hole, or you're burnt in a gas oven. To me, when life is ended, it should be like a magician's trick – you're gone with a puff of smoke hanging in the air for a couple of seconds. You're off without any of the palaver – vanished into thin air. I know people will cry and be really sad when I go. But, oh, just to get it over with. Who will turn up? What will happen? I suppose when I'm dead that won't worry me. When you know it's imminent, sometimes it's impossible for your mind not to wander and bombard you with all these questions that there really aren't any answers to.

Chapter Twelve

I MOVED to Alnwick a few months before writing this, away from the farm at last, and I'm starting to get a bit of independence. Alnwick's a lovely Northumberland market town, and there's plenty going on. I've always been coming back and forth here, and it's always felt like home. I just feel right here. I feel settled. So now I live in my own specially-adapted bungalow with two professional carers to help and look after me. It's magic. I'm sorted – living in my own place and doing what I want. It's great being in control (to a degree).

I couldn't have stuck around in Rochester. Not being able to get out, not seeing anyone for long periods of time, rarely having visitors. Stuck in that tiny cottage getting little or no stimulation. I felt I was slowly going mad. Then Ruth and Keith decided to close the café and move away, and the pub burnt down, too. Can you believe it? There was even less for me to do up there.

Then, to top it off, we found that Mindy the Yorkie had a tumour and had to be put down. That hit me hard. First Terbie, now Mindy. When you have a Yorkshire terrier, it's like constantly having a baby around, and she'd been with us for such a long time. Pets never argue with you or fall out with you – they are friends regardless, without a bad bone in their body. Having your friends put down isn't a nice thing, and you soon run out of friends.

Aye, it's been a bit of a sad old story. But guess what? It gets sadder. After 36 years of scrunching me up, my body is getting closer than ever to turning me into a ball. My ears are folding into my head, trapping liquid in there that gurgles when I try to sleep. Most of my hair has gone, and my head is covered in scabs – thank God for my white cap. My hands are now worse than they have ever been – wrists bending right over and bulging – and now my neck has started playing up. If I go on much longer, it's gonna pull my head down into my chest. My feet hurt like hell, too, and I'm finding it harder and harder to walk. But, hey, a lot has happened in the last few months and it hasn't all been bad.

Mick and Willie are my carers today, and they're a God-send, although I don't tell them that. Not long ago I took Willie to Amsterdam, and we ended up right in the front row of a sex show. It was amazing. I know I can't have sex or be touched, but there is nothing wrong with looking. And boy, did I see some things that day! Just because my appearance is not considered to be normal, doesn't mean I'm that different on the inside. I just couldn't live without my carers. At times I make their lives hell. I can swear and shout, cry and curse and they're always there taking it on the chin, because I can be such a sod when I'm not well. They have the patience of saints. They have been great for Mother, too, because she can go off and have a bit of freedom for herself at last, safe in the knowledge that Mick and Willie know how to handle me. Of course, she always steps in when they're on holiday or away on a training day.

This last year my whole life has turned around. I have guests. I entertain. I have many friends. Oh boy, do I have friends. If I could mention them all I would, but it wouldn't be fair because if I missed someone out they'd be hurt so I guess its best not to try. I have to mention Rupert and his family though.

Ru has the family title now and is known as The Rt Hon Lord Redesdale. He lives in London and sits in the House of Lords, but he's still just 'Ru' to me. I've known him since we were teenagers together in Rochester and we've had some great times. I recall when we were in Hexham together and I asked him to give me a push in my chair and let me freewheel down a hill. We ended up getting caught by a policeman who gave us a right ticking off.

Ru phoned me only the other month to talk about a speech he was making in the House of Lords, and we argued like an old married couple as I tried to get him to give the Beano comic a mention – that's how absurd our conversations are. His whole family have been good to me over the years, and I bless them. Oh shit, I sound like the Pope! But they'll understand.

I also have to mention Louise and Simon. They are just the best friends ever. We meet at the MetroCentre for lunch and I invite them to birthday meals and we contact each other regularly. There are such a lot of other people to thank for being in my life, but like I said earlier, I just can't mention them all.

One of the main reasons for moving to Alnwick was so friends like Rog have no excuse not to visit. Getting to Rochester was difficult for him, but now he visits quite often and always manages to make me laugh, which is one hell of a job when I'm down. He's been helping me write the story of my life. We started it mainly for me to get all the angst out of my system that had been building up over the years. The trouble is, creating such a thing can only happen when I'm well enough to talk. That's why it has taken so long – me lying on the couch in the living room laughing my head off while Rog is on the computer in my bedroom laughing his head off too, with both of us communicating through cordless phones. Then he'd have a drink and stay the night.

It's always been great just sitting around and putting the world to rights and it has been therapeutic, because talking and telling stories now has a purpose.

I remember once, long ago, when Rog visited Rochester with a friend called Sarah and her young daughter. They picked me up in their car and we went out for the day to Kelso on the Scottish borders, where there's a huge castle that's open to the public. We parked the car and went to check it out. I got into my folding chair and they pushed me to the main entrance. Within no time at all we were in a long queue waiting to pay when I noticed a sign informing us we could get in cheaper as a family.

I whispered to them, when no one was near us, that we should take advantage of this since together we looked a bit like a family, and they nodded their agreement. Moments later, while Rog was paying for our tickets and with everyone in the queue looking at me as they tend to do, I called out loud and clear, 'Daddy, Daddy, why do you keep hitting me?'

Well, there was an absolute stony silence from those in the queue and from the two women selling tickets. All that was missing was the tumbleweed rolling past. And if looks could kill, Rog would have been a goner there and then. Luckily, I know his sense of humour. He turned to look at me, at Sarah and her daughter, then back at me, and replied, 'Shut up, you little bugger, or I'll clip you around the ear!'

He picked up our tickets from the counter, amid gasps of horror from those around us, took control of the chair, and off we went towards the castle. We were all bursting with laughter on our way through – I could have almost split my sides. It didn't stop there. In every room we went into on the castle tour everyone else just cleared out of our way. No one wanted to be near us, or at least Rog. It was great because it meant we could get my chair everywhere without any bother. Even in the café afterwards, everyone moved away from us. What the heck? We had a good day and Rog made it out of there without being lynched.

Returning to Kelso, you go through a wooded area down quite a long, steep drive. And, of course, no one was there either... and I never let up. So as we went, I asked Rog if he would give me a push and let me freewheel, since my (real) father was always scared to let me loose and enjoy myself.

'You sure?' he asked.

'It'll be a bit of freedom I've never had,' I cajoled. 'Go on!'

'Ok then,' he replied, before giving me a push.

It was great. I picked up speed and raced away from them, singing my head off. 'Yippee, *Yippee!*'

Before long, Rog was up alongside me running, red-faced and panting. He later told me how dangerous it was and how foolish he'd been to listen to me. He'd felt terrible

seeing me race away from them like I had and was frightened in case the chair tipped over, scared that if he touched
it to slow me down, I'd tip over. As it happened, gravity took
control and the chair and I slowed down naturally. I was
fine. However, Rog was panting like an old boiler. That was
a good day for Jonny Kennedy.

I've been a very busy man over the last few months, and my
rota has taken a right hammering. I've been all over doing
stuff for DebRA, meeting people, and all kinds of things. I
now have a super fab electric chair that does everything and
anything a human could want, and an even better drive-in
bright yellow van specially built for the chair and me. So
now I can travel all over the place with Willie or Mick
taking care of me.

There's a guy called Robin who works for the Scottish
arm of DebRA. He's an unbelievably enthusiastic guy, who
invites me all over Scotland to official events to accept
cheques on behalf of the organisation. I must admit I like
that. I feel it's only right that, if someone is donating money
to a charity, they should see what they are putting it into
and where it is going. So that's it, really. Doing it has filled
many of my days and given me a purpose: going to dinners,
talking about the condition, raising awareness and money,
while helping people understand and maybe reflect on their
own lives. For a while it was like being a professional

raconteur. I've met so many interesting people, and celebrities, too, and sometimes I even feel like one myself because so many people recognise me. It's great when someone goes out of their way to come and talk to me. I've met Henry Cooper a couple of times, Simon Weston, Anthea Turner... too many to remember.

One of the most amazing people I met was Princess Diana. I received an invitation from the Palace (as you do) to go to a garden party in the summer of 1993. She was a grand lady, very nice to talk to, and she actually cared. She wasn't just listening for the sake of photograph opportunities, as there were no cameras allowed in Buckingham Palace. I wish I'd got a snap of her and me together; I thanked her for her patronage and told her how she was such a help to the charity. She was absolutely wonderful.

Within six months of moving to Alnwick I began feeling ill, drained. We flew down to London and I was diagnosed as having skin cancer. *Ye Gods!* What a kick in the bollocks. On top of everything else, you wouldn't think it possible. That was September 11th 2002, a day I'll never forget. I'd just got my life together, everything was happening, and then – *bang* – there's another bullet in the head for Jonny Kennedy.

Of course, having treatment for cancer, chemo or radiotherapy, would be out of the question since that alone would kill me, but I was offered it all the same. I decided to do without any treatment and just take it on the chin as I did with everything else that had happened to me. I just tried not to worry about it. Not much stops me in my tracks, and cancer wasn't gonna be any different. But it was still a bloody nuisance.

The cancer was pretty advanced, and the doctors told Mother that even those who received treatment only lasted a year, so there was no hope for me at all. Poor Mother. She was so upset by the news. It's hard to imagine what it must have been like to be with me through all the hurt and pain, having to watch her son go through all that, only to find out that he now had cancer.

When we left the hospital, we had a stroll along Westminster Bridge and Mother asked where I wanted to go. There was no reply – I couldn't find any words. I had the breeze and the sun on my face and there were no words that could have been spoken. Mother knew that, but that's what mothers do – try to busy themselves with something when faced with the unthinkable. When we got back home, I went out and bought a giant cuddly stuffed tiger to cheer her up. Mothers aren't meant to see their children go first.

The cancer has grown over the months, and is draining the life out of me. What can a fella do, eh? It's on my left wrist. When the bandage is off, the tumour looks like a wrinkled brain the size of a large egg. You could easily be physically sick at the sight of it. And it smells, too – worse than any smell I've ever produced, and so powerful. I hate it. I have the lads spray the new bandages with Febreze fabric refresher to mask it so it doesn't upset anyone. Nevertheless, life goes on, and we turned my bungalow into an Aladdin's cave for my first Christmas in Alnwick.

Life has moved on for Mother too. She now has a new partner, and they stayed over on Christmas Day. Simon and his wife Julie, who now have three boys, also came over for Christmas. We all had a great time, and I adore their kids. Then, at New Year, Willie took me to the local pub and on to someone's house afterwards where I think I drank everyone under the table. I can't say I was the last one standing, since I can hardly stand these days. But I was triumphant as the last one conscious.

One weekend, Rog was goading me into telling him more stories when he came up with a gem of an idea to make a TV documentary of my life. He knew someone in the industry, an editor at Tyne Tees Television, so off he went to see if he could fix things. He returned with the editor Peter and his friend Patrick, a local film director. Rog stayed in the kitchen after introductions were over, to allow them to get to know me a bit. I think I blew them away. I know they'd never seen anyone like me before, so it was almost a forgone conclusion something would be done, so I let them get on with it. Rog took a back seat with his writing and kept out of the way while I worked with Peter and Patrick; he knew I had only so much energy. They made a short film about me and pitched it to Channel 4, who commissioned Patrick to make a documentary of my life.

I had a whale of a time during the shoot. I have Rog, Patrick and the film crew to thank for that. I was worried they might just want me to sit on my bed and lie down and die with a camera stuck in my face. But, really, it was great. They filmed me all over the place doing lots of different things, and I met some fabulous people through doing it. I even went up in a glider flying across the skies of Northumberland as part of it. It was fabulous. It was *grand.*

At one point, Patrick filmed Rog and me visiting the Hoppings, Europe's largest fun fair, on Newcastle's Town Moor. That was an entertaining afternoon. We even won a couple of Pooh Bears to take home, and Mick my carer did his macho thing by showing a group of teenagers how to punch a boxing ball. The maddest part was when Patrick and I went to see a gypsy to see what she had to say about me and my condition. Apparently, she was Gypsy Rose Lee's great, great granddaughter. It was really funny trying to get into her caravan with the equipment and my chair, but we managed it. Once in there, Patrick was struggling to sit down with the camera and not to get in the way, but he managed to keep it all very natural – until he knocked over and broke her glass table lamp. When we came out, Rog asked, 'Did she say "don't worry about knocking over the lamp" before it happened?' Boy, did we laugh!

While filming the documentary we went down to London to mark DebRA's 25-year anniversary by releasing butterflies, representing beauty emerging from a crappy peeling chrysalis, in Hyde Park. It was there that I met Nell McAndrew, who had come along to represent the charity. She was lovely; an absolute vision. She was quite upset at seeing someone like me. I don't think they had prepared her, although to be honest, I don't think it's something you can prepare for. I could see she was shocked, so I made light of it and she began to smile.

She was a very nice lady. The film crew asked if I fancied her − well, what's not to fancy! And I'll let you into a secret: a bonus of being in a wheelchair is that women have to lean over to talk to you − and I could see right down her T-shirt! But it was great to meet her. It was grander than grand. She told me her sister lived up near the MetroCentre in Gateshead, so I told her I was having my housewarming in July and she should get herself along. I don't miss much, me. I said I'd get some red wine in for her, completely turning on the charm. She took my phone number − the guy's a pro!

A photographer wanted a picture of Nell giving me a kiss and, being me, I couldn't let the opportunity pass. I played around so he'd have to take the shot a few extra times: 'Have we got it this time? No? We'll take it again! We could be here a while!' What a fella I am!

Of course I didn't stop there. I really went for it with the old sob story. I told her that Mother just wanted to give me a hug but she couldn't. 'I miss out on a lot, you know?' I said, 'but it's just life.' That was it. She burst into tears. Works every time! 'I'm used to it,' I said. 'I've had 36 years of living with dressings and sores. But I know, one day, with the help that you've given, and others, that this will be history, and people won't have to suffer like this. You're making a big difference.'

Nell did come to the housewarming, and brought her mum – and some presents – along too. It was great to spend a little bit of time with her. I was so thrilled that she had taken the time to come to my little home in Alnwick. It made my day, and made Mick's day too, who was slavering all over her!

It was the garden party to end all garden parties. It was great to get everyone together, because you never know if it might be the last time. Death will be a freedom, an escape, but I will miss everyone. I'm going away, and they can't come with me, for a good while anyway. Part of accepting that you're gonna die is accepting that you're gonna have to say goodbye. So my garden party became a leaving party.

Andrew, my oldest friend, came along, plus all the gang

I knew from Rochester, Ru and his family, Rog, and many others. The bungalow and garden were buzzing with people. Mother even had a huge cake made in the shape of my bungalow with sparklers on it. Simon, Julie and the boys were great that day too. They worked so hard and there was so much food for everyone. I will miss the boys when I go. But hey, they won't be boys for long.

When it was all over, and everyone had gone home, Rog, Willie and I sat and got drunk. It was a heavy night and Rog looked like hell the following morning. He's a real character, that guy. He'd arrived at the party wearing a life-sized mask of my face that he'd made on his computer. I hated it, seeing myself. He sensed that and took it off. He's as bad as me and never misses a trick. Still, it was a good day and I was absolutely chuffed that everyone made the effort to come and see me, and give me the chance to say goodbye.

It was important to me that I organised my own funeral, chose the music and who would speak at the event and on my behalf. It all had to be sorted. I got Simon in on it, and also Beanie from the Spiritualist Church, who Mother asked, and Robin from DebRa. We arranged for the Back-worth Male Voice Choir to sing at the service, and I asked Rog to wear his most colourful shirt. Then I went off to the Houses of Parliament to persuade Ru to say a few words.

They do lovely soup down there, you know?

Next, Rog and I went along to a factory to choose my own coffin. That was a laugh. Patrick and the guys came along to film the whole thing, too. We had such a good time that day. I intended having a cardboard one like Uncle Bob, but when we saw them on display next to the wooden ones, they just looked like... well, cardboard boxes! If they could have embossed the cardboard with a design I'd probably have bought one right there and then – but a cardboard box on its own? No! The wooden ones were far better.

The young owner showed us around his factory, and we got to see his staff make my coffin, following the whole process, cutting and shaping the sides, top and bottom. Rog even tested the base for my feet, to check I'd be comfortable in it. Then I got to choose the material for the inside, checking the colour and material, as if it mattered.

Next, I had to decide what to have engraved into the wood. When the owner asked for ideas, I told him I wanted a tin of Heinz Beans on the side. He wasn't sure how to take the comment. I said I wanted people sitting at my funeral, nudging each other going, 'What does the Heinz Beans signify?' It was just something to get them talking – it didn't signify anything at all. The whole thing was strange and a bit macabre. But it was also fun. I also had them engrave a tiger on the coffin – had to have my favourite symbol on there.

'Where would you recommend I keep it?' I asked them when the coffin was finished, 'cos I'm not using it straight away.' I ended up putting it in the shed. In fact, it was there in the shed when I held my garden party, but not many of my guests knew that!

When things got too bad for me to bear I was put on morphine again, but I had to stop it. I began looking forward to it too much. It certainly gave me a good night's sleep – best I'd had for the first time in I don't know how many years. It blocked me up though. And going to the toilet was bad enough without that, which was why I stopped taking it. It's not like I wasn't used to pain and discomfort anyway. I have to apologise to Mick and Willie for having to put up with grumpy old me when things weren't going my way.

It takes them a good hour to put me to bed at night, because things have to be done slowly to prevent trauma or pain. Then the same has to happen again in the morning when it's time to get me up. Remember, they can't touch or lift me. I have to do it myself, slowly, that's why it takes so long. It's a tiring and harrowing job and doing it without morphine has become unbearable.

When I first came here, just over a year ago now, I could walk – well, hobble – with my bent legs to my bedroom. Then, when I couldn't manage that, they began to wheel me through to the bedroom on the computer chair, until I got a proper wheelchair to do the job. These days, the pain is so bad that even to stand would be like standing on crushed glass, so I don't do it.

This is the end. I just know it. And now I'm looking forward to it. It'll be like finally being free... freedom for all who are involved with me, especially Mother.

Now there is Rog and all the work he's been doing on the writing. We are nowhere near finishing that because there's so much more to Jonny Kennedy and so many more people and stories in my life to cover, but that's all gonna have to stop now. It'll be nice to be able to leave my mark. To have my story make an impact on one person alone will be grand, so to reach more than one person will be amazing.

I know the Jonny Kennedy story is reaching the end though. My energy is just progressively sapping and my enthusiasm and humour wavering... I have to soldier on. I've gone through life like that. I'm not really frightened of death, but I guess that's not surprising considering I've been waiting for it for so long. Woody Allen once said he wasn't afraid of dying; he just didn't want to be there when it happened. I can understand that. It's not death that's frightening; it's the way you go that's the worry. To me, what's meant to happen is meant to happen, so why worry about it? You can't put it off. People tend not to talk about it, and I think that's a shame because death is part of life. It's something everyone will experience – you can't hide from it forever.

So I'm just about sorted now. But there's one last job I feel I must do. I'm off my food, such as it is, and because of that I've no energy left. I find myself moving in and out of consciousness. But the film crew and I have been invited to Downing Street to meet the Prime Minister's wife, Cherie Blair. This is the last job, the one I *have* to do. I know being filmed at Number 10 will raise awareness of EB and bring in a lot of money for the charity to help find a cure. I just have to go regardless of how I feel – it's for the others I'm doing it, not me. Mother doesn't want me to go, Patrick doesn't want me to go, no one does. Willie is keeping quiet as usual, although I know he doesn't think I should go either. But I can't not go, can I?

So we went down to London, me, Willie and the film crew. I slept most of the way. We stayed in a hotel, but I can't remember much of that. I can't recall much of the next day, either, or how I even got to Number 10. I was wheeled in and shown around and met a few people before meeting Cherie Blair. I do remember her asking me if I'd been to Number 10 before. I replied, 'No, and I'm not coming back either.'

They say I died on the train going home. But I know when I died. Hell, I'd been planning it for long enough.

Epilogue
by Roger Stutter

***

I T wasn't my intention to write anything about myself, because I wanted this to be all about Jonny, which it is. But he's gone now, so I guess I have to tie up a few loose ends.

I've known Jonny since he was a teenager. However, you couldn't get to know Jonny as a single unit, you just couldn't. Jonny came as a package with his family, and over the years I got to know them all very well – Edna and Frank, and Simon and his wife and kids.

Edna is an attractive lady. When I first met her, she had long hair classically tied back in a bun. She is a spiritual seeker, a loving mother and a hard working lady with a farm to run. Frank was also a spiritual seeker, and health-conscious with weights, bars and body enhancing machinery in one of the barns, who would do anything for anybody. Simon was all grown up when I met him, living with Julie and their three boys. Together they were a caring, loving family who accepted me as a dear friend.

Don't ask me why I became so close to Jonny, I really don't know. It was nothing to do with his condition or his special circumstances. It was just as if I was drawn to him like a magnet. We were friends, and Jonny started to ask me to help him out, and it grew from there.

In those days, I'd leave my home in Newcastle and go off and spend a few days at a time up in Rochester. It was fabulous being in the wilds near the Scottish Borders after the hustle and bustle of the city. In the mornings, before Edna went in and got Jonny up and ready for the day, Frank and I would head for the hills with the dogs, and spend hours walking and climbing. It was great. But who was running the farm while we were out enjoying ourselves? Edna, of course. She'd be up early, seeing to the chickens, milking the goats, chasing the sheep and grooming the horse, while we were away. I often felt guilty about the amount of work she had to do, but it wasn't my place to interfere.

I have fond memories of those times visiting the Kennedys, calling around with friends, taking Jonny out for the day, going to the pub with him, hanging out down in the café on the main road to Scotland, or sitting in the little house Frank had made for Jonny from one of the barns.

I liked Frank. He was a really nice, smart man. But he could not come to terms with Jonny – or Jonny's condition. He needed to be away, to be anywhere rather than with his son, and would often go off somewhere rather than be faced with changing a bandage or helping him. Together we'd sit up on the hills during our morning walks, looking out across the wilderness, while he talked about his life and about his feelings and his love for his wife and his two sons. Poor Frank. He couldn't believe he had produced this beautiful boy who was in such pain whom he couldn't help, and he hated himself for how he felt and how he behaved towards Jonny.

Personally, I think that was probably what got Frank in the end – the pressure he was living under and the mental anguish he constantly created for himself over his feelings towards Jonny, just got too much for him because he didn't want to feel the way he did. He just couldn't help it.

I didn't always find it easy to deal with Jonny's condition myself. I had one of the strangest experiences of my life while staying in Rochester, which I didn't tell Jonny about for years. I was staying in a small caravan in the field tucked away out of sight to the side of the farmhouse, and I was getting ready to go out for a drink with Jonny (being lads an' all) down at the First and Last. But, while I was having a wash and shave, this sudden fear descended upon me. Out of the blue, and for no logical reason I could think of or understand, I became afraid of Jonny. I couldn't bear the thought of being near him, speaking to him, smelling or touching him. I didn't want anything to do with him. It was totally out of character. Totally not me. But I couldn't get rid of the awful feeling inside of me. I was shit-scared of meeting with Jonny, the friend I had known for so long.

I began to shake, and my mind began to think of ways of getting out of going to the pub. I finished getting ready, very slowly, but I couldn't put it off any longer. I took a deep breath, closed the caravan door, and began to walk, slowly, across the field. I was in such a terrible state. There, in the middle of the field, I shouted up into the big blue summer sky, 'What's going on here? For pity sake, help me! I can't bear this!' Suddenly, like magic, my fear disappeared. In a flash, all the crap about being afraid of Jonny was gone. All that rubbish. I felt great, confident, and happy to be alive. I breezed into Jonny's kitchen, perfectly calm, and there he was, happily waiting for me. Good old Jonny. I promised myself I'd never let anything like that ever happen again, and I went for a drink with my mate.

Jonny had a kind of sixth sense, created, I imagine, because he didn't have ninety percent of the senses and experiences fit humans have. He never went into the kitchen in his little bungalow, except when he was wheeled or carried through it on his way to the car or the bedroom, but that man knew where everything was in every cupboard. One time when I stayed over in the spare room he asked me to make him a roux. Well, I don't even own a cooker. Make a roux? I couldn't even spell it, never mind cook it – whatever *it* happened to be. However, Jonny knew where everything was and he'd shout his instructions from the couch in the living room... even telling me I wasn't stirring it correctly. And if you moved anything or put something in a different place – even though he never went there – he knew it. One day I was in the kitchen when I saw the dishcloth. It was manky and torn with holes everywhere.

'What the hell is this?' I asked Jonny's carer, holding it up to show him. He just shrugged his shoulders and shook his head. 'I'll throw it away.'

'Leave it alone. It still has a couple of months' life in it yet!' came Jonny's voice from the next room.

I smiled and whispered. 'I'll chuck it away when he's asleep. You can blame me if he notices anything. Knowing him he'll probably tell it's a new cloth by the sound of the dishes being washed.'

'I can hear you, you know!'

The following weekend, I was back in Alnwick and had bought Jonny some flowers for his house to cheer him. up. There's quite an uphill trek from the bus station to the bungalow, so you have to grit your teeth and just go for it. Just when you think you've reached the top of the hill, lo and behold it goes on and up again, then some more. I just hated that hill. I would begin the journey all smart, cool and clean, and end up like a bag of rags by the time I walked through the door. Jonny liked flowers though; their smell, their colours. I think he was hooked on the perfection of Mother Nature, more so because of the wicked cards she had dealt him.

So, this day, I arrived dishevelled as usual. The sun was shining and Jonny was in a good mood. The flowers put him in an even better mood and we had a good day. We reminisced over Uncle Bob's recent demise... the bashing of his head on the door and how rigor mortis had set in. We were both in tears of laughter, but within half an hour we were just in tears. Jonny needed the bandages changed on his wrist where the cancer was because it was getting a bit... well, *shit* was pouring through it. He called Willie in from the kitchen. I sat down on the soft foam lounge chair and watched helplessly as my friend writhed and screamed in pain. Willie put a tissue on Jonny's free wrist, because his nose always ran like a river when he went through a bandage change. Jonny lowered his head to the bandage and slowly undid the knots with his fragile teeth. On cue, his nose began to run. As he dealt with that, Willie unravelled the manky bandages delicately and carefully. I had the urge to put my arms around Jonny and comfort him, but pulled back in case I actually did, for there would be no comfort in that – except maybe for me.

Then, there in front of us, sat the culprit in all its glory: the cancer on his bent and twisted, scorbutic fleshy wrist. It sat open to the air. To me, it looked like a walnut, but much larger, and it had a smell, too. Its own unique frighteningly disgusting stench that I felt for sure was not of this world – it was death. Mix that with the odour of the puss Jonny produced – the gunge – and you've got some devil of a concoction that is almost unbearable to smell. And the room was full of it, making it difficult to breathe. And still Jonny's nose kept running, and again I wanted to hug him. Tears welled up in my eyes. Willie cleaned up any puss before attempting to put on new bandages. This was where the art of it came in. To reduce trauma, the bandages had to be put on in a certain way and were different shapes, too. Willie had them ready and had already sprayed the top ones with Febreze – then something went wrong. I don't know what it was, but the bandages weren't going on right and Jonny began to scream and rock back and forth with pain.

'Willie, what the fuck are you doing? Fucking Hell, Willie, get it right *please*,' he begged, sobbing, his nose running, while Willie attended to his wrist.

Willie was an angel. He just let all that crap wash over his head as he went through it once more, and got it wrong again.

'*Willie!*'

Jonny was still rocking backwards and forwards, wailing, *pleading*. The smell was appalling and I was on the verge of a mental meltdown when it all came right. The bandaging was over, and that bloody thing was out of sight for another couple of days. I could hardly believe it. I was exhausted, and yet I had done nothing. Only half an hour previously we were so happy, and now this? Thank God, it was over. Jonny couldn't run away from it though – he was trapped by this every day of his life.

Years previously he'd suggested I become his carer, because we got on so well. I know I couldn't have gone through that – through what Willie had to put up with and what Edna had put up with for nearly 37 years. I'd have been a piece of jelly on the floor within a day. So, selfishly, or thankfully, I didn't go down that road. I know Jonny counted Willie, Mick and all the others he'd had over the years, and not forgetting Edna, amongst his angels.

I must tell you, Jonny was no saint. He could be bloody-minded and awkward just like the rest of us. Whether it was his condition, or because he felt so helpless, I don't know. If things didn't go his way he would get depressed. I remember losing some work on the computer once. I'd pressed the wrong key and most of what we had done that day was gone. And, although I told him I could probably claw it back and recall most of what we'd done, he just sank into this place where even my humour couldn't reach. The whole atmosphere in the bungalow changed totally, to such a degree that I gave up and just had to go home. But those poor carers and, I guess, his mum had to live with that whenever things didn't go the way Jonny wanted them to.

I visited a week later and he was still in that dark place. However, I rode it out. I took him more flowers to cheer him up, and then we went to spend the day in Newcastle. He hired a chair from Shop Mobility so he could get around better, and it was a lovely day. At one point we were sitting on Northumberland Street when a gypsy lady came over to us, and promptly told Jonny he was going to live until he was 86! He looked at me, and I looked back at him. 'Not bloody likely!' he said, as we both burst out laughing. She wandered away, confused. Jonny was back to his normal self.

We all knew Jonny was dying. We had all been preparing for it for quite some time. But still, it was heartbreaking when it happened. It was 26th September 2003. I got the call and caught the bus to Alnwick to see him, stopping off at a flower shop to buy a large bunch of pink and white lilies, the ones that smell really strong, along the way. They were for Edna to take home to Rochester, so when she got up the next day the house would be filled with their beautiful aroma.

When I got there, Jonny was in his coffin in the bedroom. He looked calm, happy, not there. I stroked his forehead, and said, 'You cheeky little bugger. Good on you,' and left.

His funeral the following week was brilliant. His white hat sitting on the coffin, the tin of beans and the tiger engraved on the coffin's side, causing the stir he imagined they would. Simon spoke so eloquently about his brother. Ru did Jonny proud by making everyone laugh, easing the tension. The Backworth Male Voice Choir stood proud, singing at the back of the crematorium and I was in my colourful shirt like Jonny had asked. Along with Edna, her partner Colin, Simon, Julie, and Jonny's three nephews, all of his friends were there, wondering what the tin of beans meant. At the beginning they loudly played Queen's *Who Wants To Live Forever?* and that crappy body slid into the oven to his signature tune *Don't Stop Me Now.* Jonny was finally free. It was just the best.

'It's a sad day, isn't it?' someone said to me.

'No, way,' I replied. 'This is the best day. Jonny had some great days and some terrible days, but this day with all its highs and lows, is the *best*.'

Patrick Collerton's documentary film, entitled *The Boy Whose Skin Fell Off,* was shown on Channel 4 and was a great success. It was watched by five million viewers across

Britain, and millions more around the world. It has won thirteen awards, including an Emmy in New York, and gongs from BAFTA, Grierson and the Royal Television Society.

After seeing the documentary, viewers donated over half a million quid to DebRA's Jonny Kennedy Memorial Fund to continue the fight. Edna received hundreds of letters from people whose lives had been changed after watching it. To be honest, it was the letters that did it for me. One lady thanked Edna and said she was sad she had never met her son, as the film and Jonny's openness about an afterlife had helped her come to terms with the death of her own child. It was wonderful that the story of Jonny's life comforted and inspired so many people out there. It healed them in a way, I guess. That's what it was all about for me.

Jonny would have loved the effect his life has had on everyone, and would have been as amazed as we all are at how things have taken off. We have set up a charity called Jonny Kennedy North East, hoping to help sufferers and carers by providing them with computers and holidays. People from all over are now involved. There's a comedian – which is great as laughing was something Jonny could do with ease, and, like the alcohol, it cut through the pain. There's a chef – who has been unbelievable in organising events and getting people together – a housewife and mother, a young singer and actress... There are even two young lads who on their own collected ten quid to give to the charity and who wanted to come onboard to help. And, of course, there are all the families of sufferers – so many good people who are all welcome.

At times, it takes my breath away, seeing their love and care, their desire to help and cause change. Jonny would love them all, too, as I know Edna and I do. If this book can raise a smile, or the profile of our charity, or help a sufferer of this evil condition, then all the tears will have been worth it, in the end.

Roger Stutter

Afterword

by Edna Kennedy

I THINK I knew there was something wrong with Jonny even before he was born. Looking back, I can remember a time when I was sure the baby I was carrying was dead inside me because there was no movement. Well, as he did on many an occasion, he proved me wrong, and came into this world a very determined character.

I had to have an emergency caesarean, which was all a bit of a shock. I can remember the surgeon saying, 'You do want to save this baby?' I nodded my assent but inside my head I was screaming, '*No!*'

Maybe it was a mother's instinct that something was very wrong; I don't know. It was two and a half days before I was allowed down to see him. He had been kept in an isolation ward for fear of infection. It was at that time that I put all my emotions into a box and closed the lid. If I hadn't, I doubt if I would have been able to cope. As a girl at school, I can remember one of my friends announcing she wanted to be a nurse, and I admired her, but said I could *never* do that. I have come to learn the word 'never' is not a word to be used lightly. I had to be a nurse for nearly thirty-seven years. There was no choice in the matter – it was something I had to do for my son.

Jonny was eight weeks old when we brought him home. He was kept in the hospital for all those weeks to give me a chance to recover from the operation and to learn as much as I could about how to handle his awful skin condition. We brought him home on New Years Eve 1966, because I had the feeling if he didn't come home that year he would not come home at all. He came home in the morning, but by the evening he was back in hospital after I panicked when I caused a very large blister while changing his nappy. A nurse dressed the blister without first bursting it and I felt that was wrong. This caused the blister to spread, but they were doing their best. I began to listen to my instincts more after that and we seemed to manage a lot better. Or at least I thought so.

The doctors knew little about the condition, and we ended up taking advice wherever we could find it, which wasn't always very good. We lived and learnt. We tried

Gentian Violet once. Only once. It's an antifungal agent used to treat injuries to the skin. I put too much of it in the bath water and ended up with a purple bath, purple towels, purple hands and a purple baby. I later discovered that you had to prepare it as a one percent solution in water and apply it to the skin by painting it on. Sometimes we joked that Jonny came from another planet, but I didn't want him to actually *look* like an alien. Believe me, it took some getting off.

I suppose at the time, fear played a big part in the way I felt. Was I doing the right thing? Was I hurting him? How long would he live? How would I cope when he did die? We must have done *something* right because Jonny survived, as you know, to almost six weeks off his 37th birthday.

The last year of Jonny's life was something of a nightmare for us all. He was so sure of what he wanted to do in that year and his positive attitude helped me to cope. Both nurses from DebRA were a Godsend. I would like to take this opportunity to thank both Jackie Hitchen and Pauline Graham-King for the wonderful support they gave us over that year.

Jonny himself would say he was a waste of space; a burden on the country, and a burden on the family. I only wish he could see the amazing reaction the documentary, *The Boy Whose Skin Fell Off*, has had on the people who watched it. Not only has it brought in a lot more money for the charity, it has raised awareness of the condition and has had a remarkable healing effect on a lot of people. It was extremely interesting having a film crew around. I have seen how a TV programme works, and just how many people are needed behind the camera in order to put a show together.

As for me, I'm doing more than I ever did before, because when you are looking after a sufferer you cannot commit yourself to anything. In some respects life is still as busy, only in a different way. I feel I have been given some freedom, although I do miss Jonny a lot. I don't miss seeing him in pain and frustrated at not being able to do the things he once was able to. Someone asked me recently how I felt now that I wasn't tied down by Jonny's condition, and the only way I could explain it was to tell them, I felt like a bird let out of a cage... well, a battery hen, actually... free, but you don't really know what to do with all that freedom.

A few weeks ago I was so busy that I said I wished life would get back to normal, until it dawned on me I didn't have a 'normal' anymore. My normal for the last 37 years had been to help Jonny to be as independent as he could be. So now I will have to create a new 'normal' for myself.

Jonny was a son I have always been proud of and it has been a privilege to be his mother.

Edna Kennedy

Jonny Kennedy North East

JKNE is a new charity based in the North East of England created primarily to follow Jonny's wishes by helping other sufferers of Epidermoysis Bullosa and their carers.

JKNE's major aim is to purchase, professionally equip and run a holiday home in Florida, and to offer all-inclusive free holidays to all members and their carers, plus free entry into Disneyland and many other attractions.

The charity also aims to provide computers to all of its members, allowing them to communicate more easily with each other and to help create a community.

JKNE holds fundraising events and runs projects throughout the North East, in schools, sporting arenas and shopping centres, and welcomes anyone keen to help.

JKNE is primarily a North East charity but its aims are far reaching, hence a website is being set up to enable interested parties to get in touch, become members, and join in with events whenever they occur.

JKNE can be contacted via their official address at:

JKNE, PO Box 1192, Newcastle upon Tyne,
NE99 4TR, United Kingdom.

For further information on how you can help or support the work of JKNE please contact the appeals team on (UK) 0191 2749056 or via www.jonnykennedynortheast.org.uk.

Registered charity number: 1119765

Also available from Tonto Press:

The Rocketbelt Caper
A True Tale of Invention, Obsession and Murder
by Paul Brown, ISBN 9780955218378
When three friends set out on a quest to build a real-life Buck Rogers-style flying machine, their obsession with the Rocketbelt 2000 shattered their friendship and set in motion an astonishing chain of events involving theft, deception, assault, a bizarre kidnapping, a ten million dollar lawsuit and a horrifically brutal murder. From sci-fi to reality, this is the incredible true story of the amazing rocketbelt.

The Burglar's Dog
Alternative Guide To Drinking in Newcastle upon Tyne
by Mark Jones, ISBN 9780955218392
A hilarious and irreverent pub crawl through Newcastle upon Tyne - STILL officially the eighth best party city in the world! Now revised and updated to include new pubs and features!

Coming soon from Tonto Press:

Stephen Miller
The Autobiography
by Stephen Miller, coming summer 2008
Stephen Miller is one of Britain's most successful athletes. Record-breaking Stephen, who has Cerebral Palsy, has won three Paralympic gold medals, plus dozens of other international accolades, in the club and discus events. A writer and poet, Stephen's inspirational autobiography tells of his struggles and triumphs, and is told with refreshing honesty and infectious humour. Stephen is currently preparing for Beijing 2008 and his attempt to win a fourth-straight Paralympic gold.

Get more details at: www.tontopress.com